MEDIEVAL CRAFTSMEN
ARMOURERS

MATTHIAS PFAFFENBICHLER

BRITISH MUSEUM PRESS

© 1992 British Museum Press
Published by British Museum Press
46 Bloomsbury Street,
London WC1B 3QQ

British Library Cataloguing-
in-Publication Data
Pfaffenbichler, Matthias
    Armourers. – (Medieval
    craftsmen)
    I. Title   II. Series
    623.441

    ISBN 0-71412-054-4

Designed by Roger Davies
Set in Palatino
Phototypeset by Southern
Positives and Negatives
(SPAN), Lingfield, Surrey
Printed and bound in
Singapore

Front cover: Armourers at work
in a forge.

Back cover: Konrad Seusenhofer
made this armour for the
Emperor Charles v as a boy.
See fig. 18.

Title page: The German minstrel
Hartman von Starkenberg
forging a helmet. The scene is
fictional, but shows us what an
early 14th century armourer
looked like.

This page: A manuscript
illumination showing armed
knights in a mass joust.

Contents

INTRODUCTION

The craft of the armourer is very ancient. It reached a very high level as early as the Roman Empire, when the Roman legions had their specialised craftsmen for the upkeep and production of arms and armour. We have very little direct evidence of armourers in the early Middle Ages, but there must always have been a number of able smiths who produced various kinds of arms and armour. Some of our medieval records go back into the eleventh century, but most of the surviving evidence comes from the thirteenth to early seventeenth centuries. However, armour changed little between the fifth and sixth centuries and the twelfth and thirteenth; when we speak of medieval armourers we can, with justice, use later written sources and illustrations to give us a picture of their work, their methods and their lives.

The great period of plate armour, the fourteenth to seventeenth centuries, hardly fits neatly into the traditional division of history into 'Middle Ages' and 'Renaissance'. In fact, the date at which the European High Middle Ages gave way to the Renaissance is arguable, and such divisions are not really helpful in any case: the evolution from one phase of social and cultural development to another was usually gradual, and contemporaries seldom felt any change of epoch. This book principally deals with what we might call the most interesting and significant period in the history of armour: the development of mail into full plate armour, and the great flowering of plate armour-making up to c.1650.

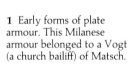

1 Early forms of plate armour. This Milanese armour belonged to a Vogt (a church bailiff) of Matsch.

THE SOURCES OF INFORMATION

Armour is depicted on medieval seals, monumental brasses and effigies, but there are considerable difficulties in interpreting these images. It is not always easy to distinguish between a formula used to depict armour in contemporary art, and the reality, unless the detail is supported by other evidence such as written sources or archaeological finds. Even then, such sources can tell us little about the men who produced the armour – the craftsmen who are the main subject of this book.

Although defensive armament made out of mail dominated the Middle Ages, surviving specimens from the eleventh to thirteenth centuries are almost unknown. The linked rings of a mail garment present such a large surface for corrosion that in the course of centuries they simply rust away. Those small fragments which have survived in various places cannot be identified as products of any specific metalworking centre. The same can be said about plate armour before the second half of the fourteenth century. Twenty-four more-or-less complete examples of coats of plate armour have been excavated at Visby on the island of Gotland in Sweden; they were buried with casualties of the 1361 Battle of Visby between the Gotland peasants and the soldiers of King Waldemar Atterdag of Denmark. Although they are certainly among the most important evidence of the transition from mail to plate armour, we cannot identify who made them.

Other surviving examples of fourteenth-century armour are rare. The earliest extant complete example is the armour of one of the Vogts of Matsch in the family armoury at Churburg, a piece of Milanese workmanship dating from about 1370. The earliest extant complete fifteenth-century horse armour was made about 1450 by Pier Innocenzo da Faerno of Milan, and is now in the City Museum in Vienna.

Fifteenth-century wills provide some evidence of the existence of certain forms of armour and sometimes of its origin, but they give us no information whatsoever about the armourers who produced it. One of the main sources of such information is financial accounts and tax records.

Another very important source is albums kept by the armourer, or by his etcher, recording the designs the armourer or etcher used with the names of the owners of the armour and the date of its production. The first important album of that group is the *Thun Sketchbook*, kept until the Second World War in the Teschen Library of the Dukes of Thun-Hohenstein. The *Thun Sketchbook* was probably some kind of pictorial record of the work of the Helmschmid family. Lorenz Helmschmid was a great Augsburg armourer who worked for Maximilian I; his son Colman and grandson Desiderius Colman continued the family tradition. Equally important is the sketchbook of the painter Jörg Sorg. He kept a book of pen drawings recording the designs he used for forty-five armours between 1548 and 1563. On most of the drawings he recorded the date and the names of the patron and the armourer. The sketchbook of Jörg Sorg is not only an excellent source for the names of all the important Augsburg armourers, it is also of great importance in identifying the names of their customers among the noble families of Spain, Italy, Germany and Bohemia. As at Augsburg, a sketch-

2 This is the earliest extant example of complete horse armour. It was made by Pier Innocenzo da Faerno, Milan, *c.*1450.

5

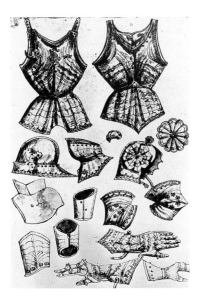

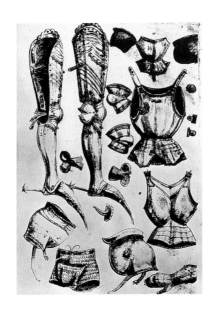

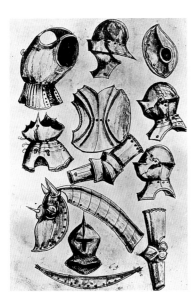

3 The Thun Sketchbook was probably some kind of pictorial record of the work of the armourer Lorenz Helmschmid.

book has survived in the Victoria and Albert Museum. The so-called *Almain Album* is the key to the study of the Greenwich Armoury. It records in pen and wash drawings thirty armours made by the Greenwich workshop in the second half of the sixteenth century. Each armour is labelled with the name of its owner, so the album offers valuable information on the clientele of the Greenwich workshop.

In the Victoria and Albert Museum in London, and in the library of the former Dukes of Braunschweig-Wolfenbüttel, two pattern books have survived. The two codices are the work of the Italian designer Filippo Orsoni. In them he painted pageant costumes, horse caparisons, different forms of armour, helmets, sword hilts, bridles and horse bits. Some of his designs are known to have been executed by the Mantuan armourer Caremolo Modrone.

The sketchbooks of the armourers provide us with information about the armourers and their patrons, but none on the making of the armour. Unfortunately, no treatise on the making of armour has survived. The sources of our knowledge are the surviving (later) illustrations of armourers at work, especially the woodcuts of Hans Burgkmair in the *Weisskunig* or the illustrations of the *Hausbuch der Mendelschen Zwölfbrüderstiftung.*

It must be stressed that we know very little about armour outside Italy and Germany in the later Middle Ages. We know a little about the armourers in the Low Countries and England, but most of our information comes from Italian and German sources. From the beginning Milan was an important centre of arms production. A street of swordsmiths, the Via Spadari, is mentioned in 1066. In Cologne we find the first evidence of smiths specialising in the production of arms and armour in sources from the thirteenth century. These mention *schwertfeger* (swordsmiths), *sarworter* (mail-makers) and *hubenschmiede* (helmsmiths). The importance of swords from Cologne is demonstrated by a quotation from the Strasbourg municipal law from 1180: *gladii qui in navibus de Colonia portantur* ('swords which are transported in ships from Cologne'). The first medieval armourer we know by name is mentioned in an Italian

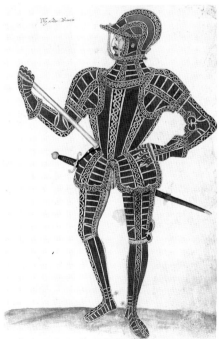

4 *Above* This woodcut by Hans Burgkmair shows Maximilian I visiting Konrad Seusenhofer in the court workshop (*Die hoffplatnerei*, 1514).

5 *Top right* The etcher Jörg Sorg kept a book of pen drawings recording his designs. This foot combat armour, etched by Sorg, was forged for Maximilian II by Mattheus Fauenpreiss.

6 *Right* Jacob Halder, master armourer in the Greenwich workshop, kept a book of pen and wash drawings of his armour, the so-called 'Almain Album'. This is now in the Victoria and Albert Museum, London. This page shows the armour made for 'My lorde Bucarte'.

document from 1232: he was Aramanno Rubei (Rossi), *osbergerii civitate Mediolani*. Rubei, a Milanese armourer, was recruited by the city of Vercello to establish a workshop for mail-making in the city. The first mail-maker from Cologne whose name we know was 'magister Rutgerus sarworter', who is mentioned several times from 1292 to 1316. In Paris the existence of mailmakers (the *haubergiers*) is mentioned in the *Livre des métiers* of Etienne Boileau (before 1260).

MAIL AND PLATE ARMOUR

Up to the fourteenth century, armament changed little. The knights of the twelfth and thirteenth centuries were armed in much the same way as the horsemen of fifth- and sixth-century Europe, with only minor differences. They wore helmets and mail shirts. The dominance of mail armour is also shown by a price decree from 1216, in which the city of Milan established the prices for mail shirts made by the *osbergeriis et panzeriis* (the Milanese armourers specialising in mail-making).

Mail was flexible and therefore relatively comfortable to wear. It offered excellent protection against sword cuts, and could also stop low-velocity missile weapons, but it could not protect the wearer from heavy, bone-breaking blows. It was necessary to wear a thickly-padded undergarment, both to cushion the body against the chafing of the mail rings and to act as a shock-absorber. It was the increasing effectiveness of the crossbow and the longbow which began to show up the deficiencies of mail shirts. A missile from one of these fearsome weapons had sufficient force to punch through mail rings. The initial answer was to make the mail rings smaller and to use double mail. However, the first really effective solution was to reinforce the mail at the most critical places with small plates which deflected blows and shots rather than absorbing them.

In 1288 the historian Bonvesi de Riva described the numerous products of the various armourers in Milan. Next to the mail shirts (the *loricas*) he mentioned *thoraces* and *lamerias* which seem to have been supplementary pieces connected with the mail. This is the beginning of

7 *Left* An armourer at work, from the 1425 *Hausbuch der Mendelschen Zwölfbrüderstiftung*. This was a sort of illustrated chronicle of medieval craftsmen, and its first volume covered 339 people and 124 years.

8 *Below* Armour changed little between the early Middle Ages and the fourteenth century. These eighth-century Frankish infantrymen and cavalrymen wear helmets and mail shirts. (From a St. Gall manuscript illumination, Stiftsbibliothek St. Gallen).

plate armour. The Dominican monk Galvano Fiamma (1298–1344) speaks in his *Chronicon Extravagans* of more than a hundred makers of *hauberks* (shirts of mail), not to mention the innumerable workmen under them who made the mail rings. This evidence indicates that from the very beginning the production of armour was a flourishing trade, but we know almost nothing of the actual organisation of a Milanese armourer's workshop of that time. The increasing importance of plate armour is shown by the Milanese price decree of 1340, in which the main item is no longer the mail shirt but the early forms of plate armour. In Cologne the *harnischmachers* (the armourers specialising in plate armour) broke away from the mail-makers and formed a separate guild as early as 1399.

As plate armour was expensive and only the very rich could afford to keep up with the latest technical developments, many knights had to be content with armour composed mainly of mail until the end of the fourteenth century. Although this book will give some information on the men involved in the business of mail-making, our main interest lies with the armourers producing plate armour. As mentioned above, the period of plate armour goes from about 1340 up to about 1650, but after 1560 there were growing difficulties in most armour-producing centres. In order to give protection against the increasing efficiency of firearms, iron *armour of proof* got thicker and thicker until it was made so heavy that it was impossible to bear its weight for any length of time. This led to a slow but steady decline in demand for armour and to a corresponding reduction in the number of armourers. So in Augsburg, one of the centres of armour production, twenty-two workshops were active in 1560 while in 1571 only nine workshops continued to produce. In 1624 only four armourers were still forging

9 A miniature by Matthew Paris, *c.*1250, showing the harness and weapons of a thirteenth-century knight. The equipment is still basically the same as that of the Frankish warriors of the eighth century.

10 *Overleaf* The Bayeux Tapestry (worked after 1077) shows Norman knights wearing helmets and mail shirts.

ETCECI

plate armour. However, it was a long time before the last armourer closed his workshop. As late as 1668 a richly decorated armour made by Francesco da Garbagnate of Brescia was presented to King Louis XIV of France by the Republic of Venice. One of the last active armourers in Europe might have been Franz Nierndorfer from Graz. He died in 1683, but his widow Anna Maria carried on her husband's workshop for some years before marrying another armourer, Hans Georg Murschön (c. 1686–88).

As in so many medieval crafts, whole families worked at the craft of armour-making and the knowledge and experience gathered by successive generations passed from father to son. Some of the great family names were: from Milan the Missaglias (real surname Negroni); the Negrolis (really Barini); from Augsburg the Helmschmids and Seusenhofers; from Landshut the Grosschedels; from Innsbruck the Treytz-Seusenhofer family.

As we shall see in the following chapters, the manufacture of armour required the skills of other craftsmen besides the armourer. After forging, the armour was still rough and blackened. It needed to go to the polisher or millman, who polished the surface with swiftly rotating wheels in water-driven harness mills. Then it went to the finisher, who was responsible for the strappings and linings, the padding and the leather gloves. In most high-quality armour the work of these craftsmen was enhanced by the decorative artists, the etchers and the gilders.

11 Armour made in 1668 for King Louis XIV of France by Francesco da Garbagnate of Brescia.

1 ARMOURERS' COMMUNITIES

When we consider the craft of the armourer in the late Middle Ages from a European point of view it is important to remember two points. One is that the production of all sorts of armament was spread all over Europe; the second is that the craft of plate armour-making (as distinct from everyday repairs and the production of the cheapest sort of munition armour, mass-produced for the common soldier) was concentrated in a few important international centres. The craft of armour-making demanded not only certain political and socio-economic conditions, but also the availability of appropriate natural resources, including an assured supply of charcoal and iron. A successful armour-producing centre also needed good access to the international trade routes and, most of all, it needed swift-flowing water to drive the heavy water-powered tools, polishing mills and water-driven hammers.

Italy and Germany were the two main centres of armour manufacture, with Italy as the leading country at least until 1500. From the thirteenth century onwards we can find traces of an important export trade in Italian armour throughout Europe. This reached its peak about 1450, when the Milanese armourers were at the height of their fame. Little hindered by guild restrictions, united in syndicates, they developed a productive capacity which practically secured them an exporting monopoly in western and southern Europe. Milanese armour was exported to England, Spain, Rhodes and Chalcis on Euböea. Several foreign rulers were so impressed by the high quality of Milanese armour that they tried to employ Milanese armourers. In 1398 the Earl of Derby, afterwards Henry IV, sent to Gian-Galeazzo Visconti for armour for his projected duel with Thomas Mowbray. Together with the requested armour the Duke of Milan sent four of the best Milanese armourers to England. We find Milanese workmen in Greenwich, Innsbruck, Landshut, Tours, Paris, Bordeaux, Bruges, Lyons and Arbois.

In Italy Milanese armourers established their workshops in Brescia, Ferrara, Modena, Mantua, Venice, Urbino, Rome and Naples. Despite this constant export of craftsmen Milan remained by far the greatest centre in Italy. In the fifteenth century Milan was able to supply four thousand armours for cavalry and two thousand for infantry within a few days of the battle of Maclodio (1427).

The great rival to Milan was Brescia. It was first promoted by the Visconti and then it became the arms factory of the Republic of Venice. We know the names of 167 armourers who worked in Brescia between 1388 and 1486. Many of them emigrated from Milan. Some, like Donato D'Arconate, even kept workshops in both cities, Milan and Brescia. We know that in 1406 the Marquis Nicolo d'Este owed 1400 ducats to Giovanni Vimercati, *armaiuolo di Milano* ('armourer of Milan'), who worked in Brescia.

The high quality of the work of some Brescian armourers is evident from the importance of their clients. Besides the Marquis Nicolo d'Este mentioned above, the Marquis of Mantua, Federico Gonzaga (1441–84), also ordered armour from Brescia; in 1479 he was a customer of a certain master Masino. The Brescian armourer Michelotti delle Corazzine worked for Federico Gonzaga and also for such high-ranking customers as the Turkish Sultan Bajesid II (1438–1512) and Guidobaldo I da Montefeltro, Duke of Urbino (1472–1508). At the beginning of the sixteenth century the armourers of Brescia were able to supply an army of six thousand men. Venetian arms production, however, was not restricted to Brescia but also had its small centres in the Friuli areas in cities like Pontebba or on the Dalmatian coast in the protectorate of Dubrovnik (Ragusa).

Florence was a lesser centre of armour manufacture, but it played a certain role, as did Genoa, the great exporting port of northern Italy. A general falling-off in the quality of Italian armour occurred in the second half of the sixteenth century and Italy finally took second place to the south German centres.

In Germany armour manufacture was concentrated in two areas: the Rhine-Westphalian district, with Cologne as the great exporting centre of low- and middle-quality German munition armour; and the south German centres, including the free imperial cities of Augsburg and Nüremberg, and the princely residences of Landshut and Innsbruck. These south German centres concentrated on high-quality armour for their noble clientele. In Cologne, where the armourers' guild split from the guild of mail-makers in 1399, there was such a huge increase in armour production that the number of water-driven polishing mills proved to be insufficient. Therefore, the city council consented to the erection of six new polishing mills in the mountainous country outside Cologne. In the expansion which followed, armourers' workshops established themselves in growing numbers in the area. Cologne remained the commercial centre of this low-quality mass-production of munition armour.

Armourers in the great south German centres worked in very small workshops and employed only a limited number of journeymen and apprentices. Especially in Nüremberg, there was always a good deal of specialisation. Every master had to qualify for a single item like a helmet or a gauntlet, which he was then allowed to manufacture. This high degree of specialisation and the easy access to the large iron-producing district of Amberg-Sulzbach, made Nüremberg famous for its munition armour and medium-quality armour. Because of the large number of small workshops it could even cope with orders for great quantities of munition armour which would be made off-the-peg. In 1362–3 the armourers of Nüremberg completed a commission for 1,816 sets of armour for Emperor Charles IV, in collaboration with the small town of Sulzbach. Because of their advantageous location, relatively near to the Hungarian border, Nüremberg's armourers profited considerably from the constant threat of Turkish invasions from the second half of the fifteenth century onwards. The city became one of the chief suppliers for the German armies fighting the Turks on the Hungarian frontier.

The Nüremberg craftsman Hermann Grünwalt is the first armourer sufficiently well recorded in contemporary documents to exist as a personality of some kind instead of just a name. He became a citizen of Nüremberg in 1434 and founded a dynasty of armourers in the city. Unfortunately, no armour known to have been made by him has survived. His son Hans Grünwalt (c. 1440–1503) must have been a highly valued armourer of his time, although again no extant work can be attributed positively to him. He worked for the Emperor Maximilian I and a number of other noblemen and princes. Like all the famous armourers, he grew exceptionally rich, owning no fewer than six houses. A great number of important Nüremberg armourers were related to the Grünwalt family: these included Wilhelm von Worms the Elder (c. 1450–1538), Wilhelm von Worms the Younger (c. 1500–71), Sebald von Worms (c. 1530–67), Valentin Siebenbürger (c. 1510–64), Endres Kolb (died 1550) and Heinrich Lochner (c. 1505–80). The leading Nüremberg armourers of the mid-sixteenth century, Valentin Siebenbürger and Kunz Lochner the Younger (c. 1510–67), included in their circle of clients members of the Habsburg family, especially Emperor Ferdinand I (reigned 1556–64) and his son Maximilian II (reigned 1564–76).

However, Nüremberg was less able to produce the fine-quality pieces for which Augsburg became famous, despite having some market for high-quality armour in Protestant northern Germany, Saxony and the Polish royal residence in Cracow. All these cities were situated on the old trading routes of the Protestant city of Nüremberg.

Innsbruck and (after 1450) Augsburg also developed into armour-producing centres which could compete with Milan. The development of Augsburg as an important centre of armour manufacture is closely connected with the rise of the Helmschmid family. The first Helmschmid recorded in contemporary documents is Jörg Helmschmid, who paid taxes in 1439. The name 'Helmschmid' means 'helmsmith'. Augsburg's first peak in artistic and technical achievement was the forging of

12 Armour for the German joust, by Valentin Siebenbürger of Nuremberg, *c.*1535.

armour for Emperor Frederick III and his son Maximilian by Lorenz Helmschmid (active 1467–1515) between 1470 and 1480. Around 1480 Lorenz Helmschmid, one of the most brilliant armourers of all time, created under the patronage of the Habsburg family the *armour garniture*: a set of interchangeable pieces to be used for all purposes in the field and in tournaments. We can see what the creations of Lorenz Helmschmid looked like in the *Thun Sketchbook*. This was lost during the Second World War, but fortunately photographs of it are preserved. This sketchbook came from the Helmschmid workshop and contained sketches and illustrations recording the armour produced there. Lorenz Helmschmid was the favourite armourer of Emperor Maximilian and the collaboration between armourer and patron was particularly fertile. In about 1480 Lorenz made an ingenious horse armour for Maximilian I. This is no longer extant, but is represented in a painting now in Vienna. The horse wears a complete barde. The legs are enclosed to the fetlocks in articulated 'sleeves'. Between 1492 and 1508 Lorenz's name appears often in the Habsburg court accounts, but he also worked for the courts of Mantua and Urbino. When Lorenz died in 1516 his son Colman Helmschmid (1471–1532) inherited the workshop and continued to work for the Imperial family, as did Colman's son Desiderius (1513–79).

We are quite well informed about the Augsburg workshops between 1548 and 1563. The sketchbook of the painter Jörg Sorg preserved forty-five armours with the names of the armourers and their patrons. Jörg Sorg records Desiderius Helmschmid, Matthäus Frauenpreiss, Hans Lutzenberger, Anton Peffenhauser, Wolf Neumaier, Wilhelm Seusenhofer, Konrad Richter and Pankraz Weiss, the cream of the master armourers of Augsburg. At this time, around 1560, Augsburg reached the peak of its fame and its dominance of the high-quality market. Colman Helmschmid and his son Desiderius were the favourite armourers of Charles V, a great customer and connoisseur. The Habsburg family's patronage provided the Augsburg armourers with a number of Spanish, Austrian and Bohemian customers. With Charles V came

14 Armour for man and horse, made for the later Emperor Ferdinand I by Colman Helmschmid, Augsburg, *c.*1526.

13 Lorenz Helmschmid of Augsburg made this armour for Archduke Maximilian (later Emperor Maximilian I) in 1480.

Spanish noblemen such as Ferdinand III Alvarez de Toledo Duke of Alba, Don Garcia de Toledo Marques de Villafranca, Claudio Fernando de Quiñoñes the Count Luna, Alonso de Osorio the Count Trastamara, Barnado Manrique de Lara and Pedro de Avila, to mention just a few. The Austrian branch of the Imperial family also brought clients to the Augsburg workshops. The Archduke Maximilian II, King of Bohemia and the Duke of Jülich-Cleve and Berg ordered their armour in Augsburg, as did the members of their court. All of them ordered great garnitures at fabulous prices.

However, Charles v's death in 1558 coincided with King Philip II of Spain's growing interest in the armour forged at Landshut, leading to a decline of business in Augsburg. As noted in the Introduction, the number of armourer's workshops declined dramatically between 1560 and 1571. Under the dominance of the great merchant armourer Anton Peffenhauser (1525–1603) the craft of the armourer survived to a certain degree, but in 1624 Augsburg had only four active armourers left and had lost its position as a big armour-producing centre.

The examples of Landshut and Innsbruck are especially interesting to study, because the courts established in these cities exercised a considerable influence on the armourers. The conditions for the development of the armourer's craft were especially favourable in Innsbruck. The first Tyrolese armourer mentioned is a master Ulrich who worked for Duke Frederick IV. He worked in Hall, a small town near Innsbruck, but Hall was evidently not a convenient place and so the armourers transferred their workshops to Mühlau. Mühlau lies at the outskirts of Innsbruck and has a supply of fast-running water to power the polishing mills. Innsbruck had easy access to Styrian iron from the Erzberg and offered the patronage of the ruler of Tyrol. Influenced by the Milanese example of Duke Filippo Maria Visconti, Archduke Siegmund (1427–96) patronised the armourers residing at Mühlau, but he did not establish a ducal workshop as did his nephew Maximilian I. The early Innsbruck craftsmen like Konrad Treytz (active 1452–69) or Konrad

15 Field armour of the Emperor Charles v, made by Desiderius Helmschmid, 1538.

16 Armour for the *Rennen*, the joust of war, made by J. Treytz in Innsbruck *c*.1490 for Emperor Maximilian I (when Archduke). It was specially designed for the joust with a large shield and semi-circular vamplate making arm protection unnecessary. The thighs were protected by two large plates.

17 Archduke Siegmund's jousting armour, made by Christian Shreiner the elder at Mühlau (near Innsbruck) between 1483 and 1484. The Archduke ordered a great number of jousting armours for the occasion of his second wedding in 1484.

Vetter (active 1452–67) had their own private workshops and had to compete for the orders of Archduke Siegmund of Tyrol.

The second generation of these Mühlau armourers, Hans Vetterlein (active 1452–83), Hans Vetter (active 1452–78), Christian Schreiner (active 1452–99), Jörg Treytz (active 1466–99) and Kaspar Rieder (active 1455–99), showed an ever-growing ability to produce elegant armour to rival their Milanese competitors. Their excellence is clear from the fact that Duke Siegmund employed them to make valuable presents for his princely relatives. In 1460 he sent an armour to King James of Scotland, and in 1465 another to his nephew Maximilian I. Gifts of armour were also sent to the Archbishop of Mainz, the Bishop of Eichstädt and King Matthias of Hungary.

In 1504 Maximilian I founded his own centre of armour production at the Innsbruck court. The highly talented Konrad Seusenhofer was put in charge and a number of masters and journeymen were engaged to carry out innumerable Imperial orders. Besides the court workshop, the private workshops of the freelance armourers at Mühlau continued to exist, despite the constant tensions between the two.

The development of the armourer's trade in Landshut was very similar to the conditions in Innsbruck under Siegmund of Tyrol. From 1253 to 1363 and again from 1397 to 1503 the city was the residence of a branch of the ducal family of Bavaria. The dukes did not establish their own workshop, but the huge demand created by their court offered great opportunities for the Landshut armourers, who preserved their skills even after the court was transferred to Munich. As in the other south German centres, the first important Landshut armourers recorded in contemporary documents (beyond the occasional mentioning of a name) are to be found in the middle of the fifteenth century. Although no pieces made in the workshops of Konrad Weiss (active 1459–93), Sigmund Paumgartner (active 1474–85) or Caspar Satzenberger (1471–95) have survived, given their circle of clients they must have been important armourers of their time. In 1476 Konrad Weiss worked for the King of Bohemia and Hungary, Duke Georg of

18 Konrad Seusenhofer made this armour with bases ('skirts' of cloth or metal) for the later Emperor Charles V, in Innsbruck between 1512–14.

19 A detail of the splendid 'Burgundy Cross' garniture made by Wolfgang Grosschedel of Landshut for the future Philip II of Spain, 1551.

Landshut and Duke Otto von Bayern-Mosbach. The only surviving armour which can be definitively attributed was made by Matthes Deutsch (active 1485–95). He produced several armours for the court of Duke Frederick of Saxony. Two of these are preserved in Vienna. In 1521 Wolf Grosschedel became a citizen of Landshut. He collaborated with his son Franz, and with the Grosschedels' workshop Landshut reached its peak as a production centre of high-quality armour. Philip II of Spain esteemed the Grosschedels' workshop at Landshut highly, ordering armour garnitures for himself and for his son Don Carlos; many of the Spanish and Austrian nobility followed his example.

Lesser centres of armour manufacture in Germany were Strasbourg, Ulm, Memmingen, Stuttgart, Vienna, Graz, Basel, Zürich, Leipzig, Erfurt, Magdeburg and Lübeck. In north Germany there was also the area of Wittenberg, which played some part in the production of high-quality armour. Next to Italy and Germany in importance were the Low Countries. From the fifteenth century they became an important manufacturer and exporter of low- to medium-quality munition armour. Bruges seems to have been one of the greater centres of armour manufacture in the Netherlands. One of the craftsmen from Bruges – a certain Pierre de Bruges – was the armourer of King Edward II of England, and a Hennequin de Bruges worked as a mail-maker in the second half of the fourteenth century in Avignon. Like all the great armour-producing centres, Bruges imported a number of Milanese craftsmen. The Rondel family had its origin in Milan. The first armourer from this family to settle in Bruges was Jean Rondel, but we know more about his son Martin Rondel. He was, like his father, born in Milan and he acquired the citizenship of Bruges in 1464. In 1467 he made a hauberk of fine mail for the Duke of Burgundy and in 1473 he worked for an English client, Sir John Paston. In 1486 he worked for Maximilian I and most probably also for his son Philip the Handsome. Another famous Italian armourer dynasty from Bruges was the du Cornet (or Corneto) family. Balthasar Corneto made several suits of armour for Charles of Burgundy between 1468 and 1470.

20 *Right* This decorated half armour was forged in one of the north German centres of manufacture. It belonged to Johann von Rantzau (1492–1565).

21 *Below* The Low Countries were important armour producers, though very few examples of Flemish armour have survived. This jousting armour was made by 'Master H' for the Emperor Maximilian I or his son Philip the Handsome, *c.*1500. It has the typical 'frog-mouth' helmet and reinforced left elbow of tournament armour.

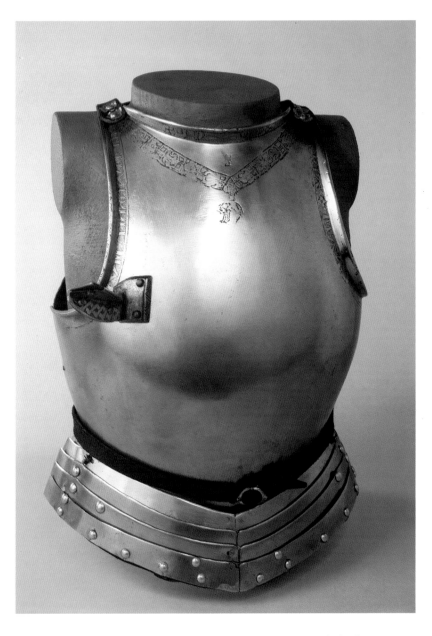

22 Breast plate of Philip the Handsome, made by 'Master H' in the Netherlands *c*.1490.

At the same time a Valentin du Cornet (Corneto) forged tournament armour for the Duke of Burgundy. Another member of the du Cornet family, Ottelin (Ottelino), played an important role at the court of the duke. He became his personal servant and his court armourer. In 1444 he made five harnesses for his master and then made three more in 1446. In 1452 he worked for the Comte de Charolais, the son of the duke. It seems that he returned to Milan, because we know of an Ottolino da Corneto who came from Milan and worked in 1465 in Ferrara.

The most important centre of armour production in Flanders was without doubt Tournai. It was the only city in Flanders where the number of craftsmen employed in the manufacture of arms and armour surpassed the number of craftsmen employed in the textile industries. In the twelfth century there were twenty-three armourers and three textile workers; in the fourteenth century 187 armourers and seventy-two textile workers. Only in the fifteenth century was the preponderance of armourers lost, with 232 armourers and 330 textile workers. In the fourteenth century the skills of the Tournois craftsmen were in great demand. A Gerard de Tournai was *heaumier* (helmsmith) to Edward III of England, and Janin de Tournai worked in Lyons at the end of the fourteenth century. Brussels, which was the preferred residence of the Dukes of Brabant from the middle of the fourteenth century, and from 1430 on of the Dukes of Burgundy, developed into an important centre of high-quality armour production. We know of no less than seventy-three armourers from Brussels. They were highly esteemed; Henry VIII sent for an armourer from Brussels, together with Italians and Germans, when he founded the armoury at Greenwich.

France, a centre of medieval culture, played a minor role in the manufacture of armour. No French city ever established a permanent reputation as a seat of armour production. Still, Paris must have been the metropolis of French armourers. Froissart mentions in his description of the battle of Rosebeque the noise armourers made in Paris. There was a *rue de la Heaumerie* in Paris in the parish of St Germain L'Auxerrois.

The *armuriers* and *heaumiers* were also located in the parish of Saint Jacques de la Boucherie. In 1516 their guild had a statue of Saint George (their patron saint) placed in the church of Saint Jacques.

Some armour was also produced in St Quentin, Noyon, Senlis, Rouen and Chambly le Hauberger. Chambly le Hauberger (near Beauvais) was celebrated for mail-making. It is mentioned as early as the eleventh century. Montauban was famous for its helmets and in the valley of the Loire Angers, Tours and Bourges became centres of armour manufacture in the fifteenth century, largely for political reasons. Under Louis XI, Charles VII, Louis XII and Francis I, the French court armourers generally resided at Tours. France imported armour from Italy in large quantities, and a great number of Italian craftsmen were employed in France. Bordeaux and above all Tours and Lyons were the centres of these Milanese 'colonies' from the early fifteenth century onwards. The most important colony was established at Lyons. Of twenty-four Milanese armourers known to have settled in France in the fifteenth century eleven lived at Lyons, ten at Tours and three at Bordeaux. Not all of them came directly from the city of Milan. Most originally came from the district situated between Lake Maggiore, Lake Como and the city of Milan. Loys de Lacques, who was brought to France in 1497 by Charles VII probably came from Lecco, on Lake Como. From the same area was Balsarin de Treytz (1474–1507) who worked in Tours. He was called in Italian 'da Trezzo' after a village next to Lecco. Jacques de Canobio, who also worked at Tours, named himself after Canobbio, a little town near Lugano. Several of these Italian immigrants settled permanently in France and founded dynasties of armourers. The family founded by Jean Merveilles (Meraviglia) of Milan at Tours in 1425 was still practising the craft 160 years later. Another of these Italian familes of artisans was the Dausonne family, which quickly became famous. The origin of the Dausonne family is to be found in the area near Lake Maggiore in Lombardy. Jehan Dausonne I was active in Bordeaux around 1485–90 and in 1523 he was the court armourer of King Francis I

at Tours, where he married the daughter of one of the king's librarians. His son Lauren succeeded him in the management of the workshop, and his nephew, Jehan Dausonne II, lived in Paris where he, too, was well known for his mastery of the craft. The two sons of Jehan Dausonne II, Jehan III and Simon, were royal armourers in Nantes, and at the beginning of the seventeenth century Jehan Dausonne IV was still active in the manufacture of armour.

South Germany also exported a large quantity of arms and armour into France, part of which came in via Basel in Switzerland and via Avignon, to the benefit of French commercial centres such as Montpelier, Beaucaire, Marseilles and Lyons.

The situation in Spain was similar to that of France. There must have been a considerable amount of armour manufacture in Spain, but almost nothing is known of it. In 1257 a mail-makers' guild existed in Barcelona and an armourer by the name of Ramon de Tor worked in Valencia. In 1308 he received an order for an armour from King Jaime II. Also we know that at Calatayud, a town near Saragossa, there was a famous workshop for helmets carrying an armourer's mark like a crow's foot. It is also known that there were armourers working at Burgos in the north of Spain and at Seville. At the end of the sixteenth century an important centre of high-quality armour manufacture was established at Eugui, north of Pamplona. Like France, the Iberian Peninsula was a large importer of Italian armour, and Italian craftsmen emigrated in considerable numbers to Spain. In the sixteenth century the influence of the Habsburg court led many Spanish noblemen to go to the armour-producing centres of south Germany for their exquisite armour.

England had its only important centre in London, where the makers of plate armour received their regulation as a separate company under the name of the Guild of Heaumers (helmet-makers) in 1347. Out of this craft guild the Armourers' Company emerged as an organised body of armourers, which received its royal charter in 1453 (see Chapter 2). The armour produced by the Armourers' Company of London seems not to have come up to the standard

23 Tonlet (skirted) armour made for Claude de Vaudrey by G. M. Meraviglia and Damiano Missaglia, Milan, *c.*1495. The Meraviglias were Milanese, but also worked in France.

of fine-quality armour produced on the Continent. Despite this, single masters like Johne Richmond, who produced armour on a large scale, became rich enough to buy the Company's land in Farringdon Street.

King Henry VIII established the Royal Workshops in Greenwich and Southwark, recruiting his armourers on the Continent, first in Italy and Flanders, then in Germany. The Almain Armoury at Greenwich developed into one of the great centres for high-quality armour.

Although York never established any reputation for armour production, the craft of the armourers was important enough for them to form a separate guild in the city in the second half of the fourteenth century.

The Swedish king established a royal workshop in Aarboga along the same lines as the Almain Armoury in England.

Very little is known about eastern Europe. Prague had some workshops which reached a certain level of excellence in high-quality work under the governorship of Archduke Ferdinand II of Tyrol. About Poland we know even less, but (at least in the fourteenth and fifteenth centuries) Cracow seems to have had an armour-producing industry of its own. During the period from 1395 to 1450, twenty-two sword-makers and thirty-two mail-makers and armourers settled in Cracow and accepted municipal rights there. In the sixteenth century Polish noblemen ordered their armour from Nüremburg, the great exporting centre for the eastern European market.

24 One of the finest products of the Prague workshops was this gilded and etched half armour for Stephen Bathory, King of Poland, made *c.*1560.

25 *Opposite* Nuremberg exported a great deal of high quality armour to Poland, like this parade armour for man and horse made for Sigismund August II of Poland by Kunz Lochner.

steel or of 50 per cent steel was subject to inspection: iron armour was not, and so never shows the city mark. In Landshut the regulations of 1479 demanded that armour should be viewed and stamped with the guild mark, but armour from Brunswick shows no mark because the armourers of that city did not form a separate guild. They belonged to the blacksmith's guild. The view marks of Augsburg and Nüremberg are probably the most commonly seen on surviving armour, though we also sometimes see the marks of arsenals which produced armour. In addition to the guild mark, the personal mark of the armourer was stamped with a punch on the surface of his finished work. This often consisted of his initials, like the MY

33 of the Missaglia or the crowned A of the

34 Armourers' Company of London. The stamps could also take other forms, such as the trefoil of

32 the Treytz or the crossed keys of the Negroli family. Sometimes marks were symbolic: for example, the helmet with a cross as a crest used

35 by the Helmschmid family.

33 The armourer's mark of Tommaso Missaglia.

34 The mark of the Armourer's Company of London.

35 The armourer's mark of Lorenz Helmschmid.

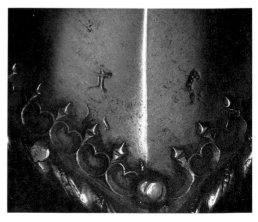

32 *Left* The armourer's mark of Jörg Treytz.

3

THE MEDIEVAL ARMOURERS: WHO WERE THEY?

THE MERCHANT ARMOURERS

In Italy, especially in Milan, the organisation of the armourers differed greatly from the German pattern. The Italian armourers organised themselves into great commercial companies, like the Italian merchants of the later Middle Ages. In Italy no restriction existed on the number of employees and apprentices one entrepreneur was allowed to employ. Besides this, in Milan we find a high degree of specialisation of a kind we can associate with mass-production. The journeymen employed by these Milanese merchant armourers often did nothing but forge the same particular part of a complete armour over and over again. The armour of Frederick I, Elector of Palatine, from the Vienna Armoury, was the product of the cooperation of a number of armourers. The most famous Milanese workshop, owned by Tommaso Missaglia (active 1430–52), was responsible for the cooperation of the different masters but this armour also bears the master marks of Antonio Missaglia (active 1441–96), Antonio Seroni (active 1450) and Pier Innocenzo da Faerno (active 1452–62).

Such cooperation was normally enshrined in a contract. In 1438 Giacomino da Trocazzano committed himself to produce *celatas* (helmets) for Giovanni de Deviziis. At the same time Giovanni da Garavalle worked just cuirasses and mail shirts and in 1423 Cristoforo Corio produced only shoulder defences and arm defences for Petrolo da Fagano. The contracts usually remained in force for two years. However, in individual cases contracts between the members of a society could stipulate a longer period. In 1485 Estienne Dausonne (active 1485–90), Ambroise de Caron (active 1485–1502), Claudin Bellon (active 1485–91) and Pierre de Sonnay formed a society to produce and sell armour in

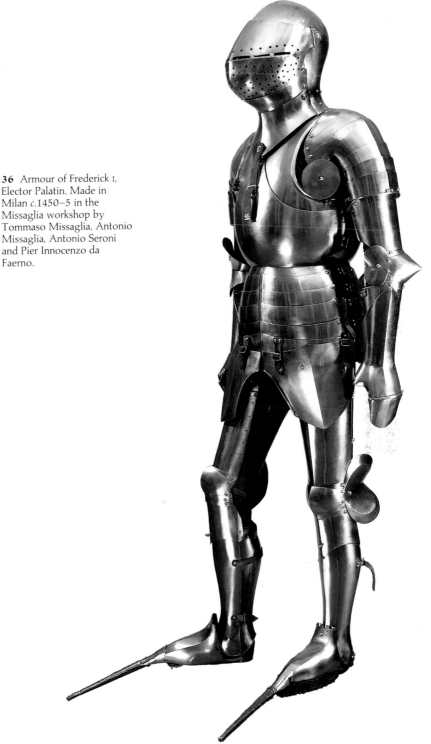

36 Armour of Frederick I, Elector Palatin. Made in Milan *c.*1450–5 in the Missaglia workshop by Tommaso Missaglia, Antonio Missaglia, Antonio Seroni and Pier Innocenzo da Faerno.

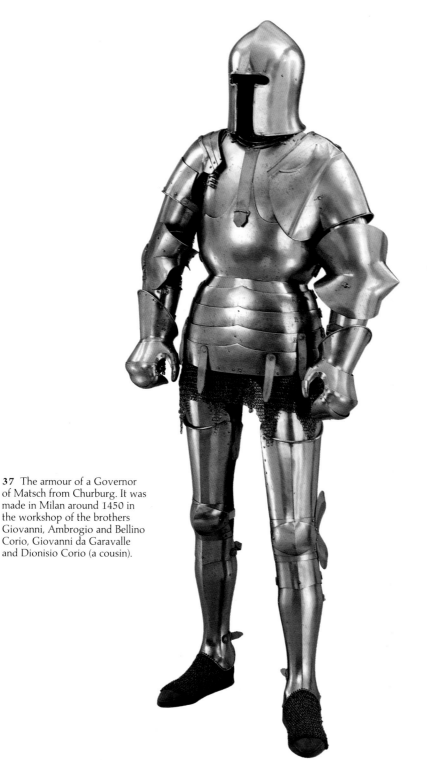

37 The armour of a Governor of Matsch from Churburg. It was made in Milan around 1450 in the workshop of the brothers Giovanni, Ambrogio and Bellino Corio, Giovanni da Garavalle and Dionisio Corio (a cousin).

Bordeaux for twenty years, but it lasted only five years.

It was not unusual for a journeyman to rise to the position of a partner. In 1423 Cristoforo Corio was still an employee of Petrolo da Fagano; three years later he was his partner. Alongside the partnerships which developed in workshops, huge trading companies existed with associates, stock funds and contracts which laid down the obligations of every associate and his share of the profit. In 1430 such a contract between Tommaso Missaglia and Bellino Corio stipulated that Tommaso had to provide money and arms worth 5,000 lire, while Bellino Corio would sell the armour in Tuscany and Romagna. This is the usual form of a contract in medieval Italy, where one contractor advanced the money and the merchandise (in this case the armour) and the other contractor did all the work. If the business was a failure the investor lost his money. If it succeeded the investor was reimbursed all the money he had advanced plus two thirds of the profit.

In a different form of contract both sides advanced money. In a three-year contract concluded in 1438 Venturino Borromeo and Matteo Marliani decided to form a society to produce and sell armour. Borromeo advanced 4,133 lire, Marliani only 2,060 lire. Marliani risked only half as much money, but he had to do all the work. Borromeo, who invested the huge sum of 4,133 lire, guaranteed his close control of the business by limiting how much Marliani could borrow.

Because of the close relationship between Milanese armourers and merchants the great armourers are often called in documents *mercanti Milanese* (Milanese merchants). The business of the big merchant-armourers could be extensive; Tommaso Missaglia was owed money by customers all over Italy and Spain. In 1436 he commissioned Gaspare de Zugnio di Milano to collect debts in Catalonia, Navarra, Sicily, the Kingdom of Aragon, Galicia and from the Master of the Order of Santiago.

The Milanese merchant-armourers had an elaborate retailing system in western Europe. One of these merchants, Francesco Datini, established himself in Avignon in 1361. He traded in arms and armour. In 1367 an inventory of his shop lists forty-five *bacinets* (a kind of helmet), three *chapeaux de fer* (iron helmets), ten *cervellers*, sixty breastplates, twenty cuirasses and twelve hauberks of mail from two Milanese armourers, Basciamuolo of Pescina and Daresruollo of Como. In 1395 Datini expanded his trade and began sending Milanese armour to Barcelona, where he expected to realise a profit of fifteen per cent. The huge volume of the arms trade is exemplified by a merchant armourer called Frederic the Lombard, who assembled the following in Bruges for the fleet of Philip the Fair in 1295:

2,853 helmets
6,309 round shields
4,511 mail shirts
751 pairs of gauntlets
1,374 gorgets
5,067 coats of plates.

In Germany guild regulations normally prohibited the formation of Italian-style big companies led by merchant armourers. But some strong individuals disregarded these restrictions. Anton Peffenhauser, one of the most important Augsburg armourers from the second half of the sixteenth century, was also one of the great merchants in arms and armour. This brought him into conflict with the guild authorities. When he had to fulfil an order from Christoph, Count of Arco, for six hundred suits of armour in twelve weeks, he imported three hundred from Nüremberg which was against guild regulations. The guild tried to fine him 600 florins but Peffenhauser's influence in the city council was so great that he could ignore the fine. He grew so wealthy that in 1556 he became a member of the great Council of Augsburg. The guild, which had no power to enforce its restrictions on him, even had to elect him to the position of a warden of the guild in 1563.

COURT ARMOURERS

The history of the great armourers' art is one of princely patronage. Only a few leading connoisseurs and customers were able to induce the outstanding masters to give of their best. The armourer's very close relationship with a royal or noble patron sometimes developed into some form of legal contract. This could vary from a contract binding the armourer to his patron and demanding preferential treatment for him, to outright employment of the armourer in a court workshop.

The earliest type of princely armourer was an entrepreneur who was under an obligation to give preference to his patron. The princely customer normally made an annual payment in consideration of his special treatment. We find this kind of relationship in Milan. When Francesco Sforza became the new duke of Milan he appointed Tommaso Missaglia and his son Antonio as his court armourers (*ad fabricandum arma pro persona nostra*). In 1475 Charles the Bold, Duke of Burgundy, made a contract with Alexandre du Pol de Milan who, in return for a yearly income of 120 ecus, a house, a polishing mill and the privilege of paying no taxes, was obliged to provide the duke with one hundred

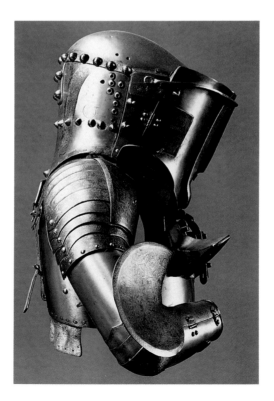

38 Armour for the joust made by Giovanni Angelo Missaglia, *c.*1490, for the Milanese ambassador at the court of Maximilian I. The Missaglia family often worked for the Milanese court, so it is not surprising that a Milanese ambassador should go back to them for his armour.

39 Foot combat armour of Maximilian I, made by Francesco da Merate in the court workshop at Arbois between 1495 and 1509.

pieces of armour. (He received an additional payment for each piece of armour he actually delivered.) Emperor Maximilian I founded a court workshop in Arbois, and persuaded Duke Ludovico il Moro from Milan to allow the armourers Gabriele and Francesco da Merate to move to it in 1495. Maximilian gave them a contract for three years. Under this contract the Merate brothers received 1,000 francs and 1,000 florins. In return for this they pledged themselves to set up a forge, a mill and workshops at Arbois in Burgundy. Gabriele was also to receive 100 francs and to be free of taxes. We don't know why, but Gabriele never went to Arbois. He most probably stayed in Milan where he continued to work for Maximilian I, because the Emperor still owed him 2,000 florins in 1506. Gabriele's brother Francesco da Merate set up the court workshop at Arbois, where it remained from 1495 until 1509.

When Maximilian took over the government of Tyrol from his uncle Siegmund he established the court workshop at Innsbruck in 1504. Although an important armourers' colony already existed at Mühlau near Innsbruck, Maximilian did not try to bind a freelance armourer to his person. He developed a court workshop following a totally different pattern. In his workshop the armourers were paid a salary plus a certain allowance for every finished work. The court workshop was intended to provide fine-quality armours for Maximilian I and to produce munition armour for his armies. To achieve this Maximilian engaged the Augsburg armourer Konrad Seusenhofer in 1504 for six years. In 1507 the court workshop set up a polishing mill on the Sill to save the journey to Mühlau. The Emperor arranged for supplies of sheet metal from Leoben, but it took Konrad Seusenhofer until 1508 to get the Imperial armoury functioning properly. When Konrad Seusenhofer renewed his contract with the Emperor in 1509 it was stipulated that he would be paid 200 florins a year and would work only for the Emperor. Under Seusenhofer's supervision would be six journeymen, four polishers and two apprentices. The journeymen were to receive 50 florins a year, the apprentices half that amount. The Emperor assigned 1,000 florins a year to the

court armoury, which proved insufficient. Because the court workshop could not handle a big order for two thousand suits of munition armour Konrad Seusenhofer had to cooperate with the armourers at Mühlau. This led to an open conflict in 1514, when the court armourers accused Mühlau of delivering inferior-quality armour which would damage the reputation of the Innsbruck workshops.

Seusenhofer directed the court workshop until 1517, when he was succeeded by his brother Hans until 1555. After the death of Maximilian I there was a crisis in the court workshop. In 1528 there was physical conflict between freelance armourers and those employed by the court. Michael Witz der Ältere (the Elder) was hindered at his work. Hans Seusenhofer and his son Jörg were threatened and hit. The authorities had to intervene. These tensions ended in the confirmed precedence of the court workshop in Innsbruck. Hans Seusenhofer was followed by his son Jörg Seusenhofer, who made the wonderful Adler (Eagle) Garniture for Archduke Ferdinand II of Tyrol. In 1567 the new ruler of Tyrol, Archduke Ferdinand, dissolved the court workshop led by Jörg Seusenhofer and dismissed him with a yearly pension of 160 florins and the post of administrator of the Innsbruck arsenal. Ferdinand II installed his personal court armourers Wolfgang Kaiser and Melchior Pfeifer in his place. This shows the close relationship between the patron and the court armourer. They were followed by the brothers Jakob and David Topf. The Innsbruck court armoury continued to exist until 1640; Christoph Krämer (active 1637–62) was the last court armourer in Innsbruck.

In 1511 the two Milanese armourers Filippus de Grampis and Johannes Angelus de Littis came to England to work for King Henry VIII in a court workshop in Southwark or in Greenwich. With them came three more craftsmen from Milan and two from Brussels, but it seems that they did not come up to the king's expectations. When Emperor Maximilian I sent an armour from the Innsbruck court armoury as a political gift to Henry VIII, the English king tried to found a royal workshop of his own following the Innsbruck pattern. Because English armourers

40 Foot combat armour from the Eagle garniture of the Archduke Ferdinand II of Tyrol, made in 1547 by Jörg Seusenhofer and etched by Hans Perckhammer.

41 Armour made for Henry VIII by Italian or Flemish craftsmen working in England, about 1515. Matching horse armour made in Flanders, but decorated in England, 1514–19.

42 Henry VIII's armour for combat on foot made by Master Armourer Martin van Rone in the royal workshop at Greenwich.

were not capable of making fine-quality armour, and the Italian and Flemish armourers were not as good as he expected, Henry VIII employed Netherlandish and German craftsmen. In 1515 he invited eleven German (Almain) armourers to work for him. He set up the court workshop under a master workman Martin van Rone, first at Greenwich, then at Southwark and finally at Greenwich again. It was these Almain craftsmen who formed the nucleus of the Greenwich School, which was characterised by careful design, functional but economic arrangement of garnitures and a love of technical devices and unusual forms.

The Greenwich armoury made armour primarily for the king and for those privileged persons who got royal warrants. The *Almain Album* is an excellent source in which to study those privileged customers. It reads like a list of the great sixteenth-century noblemen at the court of Queen Elizabeth I: Lord Pembroke, Lord Worcester, Lord Buckhurst, the Earl of Cumberland, Sir James Scudamore, Sir Henry Lee, Sir John Smythe and Sir Christopher Hatton. This concentration on fine-quality armour enabled the Greenwich workshop to maintain an extraordinarily high standard. The German armourer Jacob Halder, whose name appears on two pages of the *Almain Album*, was master workman in Greenwich from 1576 until his death in 1607. He came from Augsburg to Greenwich in about 1553–4. The English court was, at that time, interested in Augsburg armour and etching, which was also preferred by the Spanish nobility. Halder seems to have mastered the technique of etching in addition to his skill as an armourer. He included sketches of his own creations and those of his predecessors Erasmus Kyrkenar (master workman 1540–67) and John Kelte (master workman 1567–76) in the so-called *Almain Album*, which today is one of the treasures of the Victoria and Albert Museum in London. Jacob Halder's successor as master workman was William Pickering (1607–18). For an armour made for Henry, Prince of Wales, the elder brother of Charles I, he received the enormous sum of £340 (in 1614).

The third royal workshop was the Royal Armoury founded at Aarboga in Sweden in 1551. Like Henry VIII in England, King Gustav Vasa imported German workmen. The armoury in Aarboga produced both fine-quality armour for the king's use and munition armour for the royal armies, as the Innsbruck workshop did.

It was not only kings who had their own court armourers. Noblemen like the Gonzaga of Mantua did too. The first documentary evidence of Caremolo Modrone da Milano (1489–1543) in the service of the Dukes of Mantua dates from 1521, when he is mentioned in a letter to the duke from a Mantuan armourer called Jacopo da Brescia. In 1528 Modrone forged an armour for the Emperor Charles V for whom he worked again in 1536. On the order of Duke Federico Gonzaga, Modrone also made an armour for the son of Don Garcia de Toledo, Viceroy of Naples. It is evident from the importance of his clients that Modrone must have enjoyed a high reputation. On his death in 1543 he was succeeded as court armourer of the Gonzaga by maestro Marco Antonio.

Only in the greatest courts would the court armourer actually make armour. Most great nobles attached a permanent armourer to their household to clean and maintain their armour and to make minor alterations and adjustments. Alongside the court workshops producing or maintaining quality armour, we often find other groups of armourers specialising in the production and upkeep of munition armour. We might call them the 'arsenal armourers' because they were often employed by the big arsenals of cities like, for example, Graz, Zürich or Venice. In Graz, which specialised in munition armour, there were three classes of armourers. First, there were the independent armourers, who worked mainly for the Graz arsenal, but had to produce at their own risk and ask for the privilege of selling their products to the arsenal. Graz was on the Turkish frontier of Austria and under constant threat of attack. Therefore it had a great arsenal of weapons needed for the defence of the Austrian frontier. The arsenal in Graz still preserves the largest collection of armour in Europe, and most of it was made locally by these 'freelance' armourers.

The second group of armourers was employed directly by the arsenal. Their main tasks

43 Ornately-decorated armour of George Clifford, Earl of Cumberland (1558–1605) made by Jacob Halder at the Greenwich Armoury. This is now in New York.

were to service and repair the stock of weapons, and to produce munition armour. They were paid 15 florins a year and their tools were supplied.

The third and most privileged group were, as usual, the court armourers who worked for the duke in Graz and were paid more than six times the wages of the armourers working for the arsenal.

A similar situation, with independent armourers and armourers employed by the town arsenal, existed in Zürich and in Brunswick. The same appears to be true of Venice; in 1566 a Venetian notary certified that G. B. Muziano and his son, both from Brescia, had worked for three years as armourers in the arsenal of Venice.

It was not only the great nobles and town arsenals that employed craftsmen to maintain their armour. We know that a small number of armourers were also attached to troops; evidence of this has been found at the castle of Chalcis, on the Aegean island of Euböea. Chalcis, a Venetian fortress, was captured by the Turks in 1470. Venetian armour found at Chalcis is of variable workmanship, and so we can assume that repairs or additions were made by the troops' armourers (probably local men) to work originally produced by the more expert armourers of Italy.

THE GOLDSMITH-ARMOURERS
In the late Middle Ages, knights spent vast sums of money on their appearance. They employed not only armourers but also goldsmiths, who produced the applied decorations for their splendid pieces of armour. From 1300 onwards bacinets were elaborately decorated in gold and silver. Although no examples are known to have survived, there is evidence from contemporary accounts that they were also sometimes enamelled and encrusted with pearls and precious stones. In his *Chronicles* of 1385, Froissart mentions that the crown on the bacinet of the King of Castile was made of gold enriched with jewels which were valued at 20,000 francs. In 1467 Charles the Bold ordered a gorget enamelled in red and black from the goldsmith Gerard Loyet. In 1513 Henry VIII paid his goldsmith Robert Amadas £462.4s.2d to dec-

orate a headpiece and a sallet with gold and precious stones. These splendid decorations were not restricted to armour for humans; horse armour could also be enriched in this fashion. When the Count de Foix rode into Bayonne (probably in 1451) his horse wore a steel headpiece decorated with goldwork and jewels worth 15,000 crowns. The value of a jewelled shaffron of the Count of St Pol was estimated at 30,000 francs.

Goldsmiths also made gold and silver mail for the decorations of helmets and gorgets. The will of Duke Philip the Good shows that he owned a mail standard (collar) made of solid gold. In 1382 Hennequin du Vivier (the King of France's goldsmith) made gold mail to decorate the king's bacinet. Goldsmiths also made luxurious buckles and rivets in silver and gold. In the household accounts of Jean the Fearless we find payments to a goldsmith Jehan Mainfroy (in 1416) for buckles and rivets of gold.

Throughout the fourteenth and fifteenth centuries goldsmiths played an important role in the decoration of luxury armour. In the sixteenth century the situation changed a little, because at that time several goldsmiths produced their own armour instead of just decorating the work of others. These pieces were highly decorated and embossed, and were bought by princely patrons. Most of these goldsmiths were Italians, but there were also at least one German, one Flemish and one French artist who made embossed armour, in a style quite distinct from that of ordinary armourers.

One of the most important sculptors of the sixteenth century, Leone Leoni (1509–90), especially famous for the bronze sculptures he made for Charles v and others, also forged a highly decorated helmet for the Duke of Parma and Piacenza in 1546. The duke was so pleased with this lost *celata belissima* (wonderful helmet) that he made Leone Leoni *maestro delle stampe delle zecche* (master of the mint). In the same year Bartolomeo Campi (active 1500–73), working in the small city of Pesaro, finished a masterly 44 Roman parade armour for Charles v (Madrid A188). Bartolomeo Campi worked as a goldsmith, an embosser, a military architect and as a specialist in every kind of military engineering.

45 Shield made by Giorgio Ghisi (1520–82) in Rome *c*.1540. In the centre is a battle scene, surrounded by allegorical figures, and other small scenes. Some of the latter depict the Trojan war.

44 'Roman-style' parade armour of Emperor Charles v by Bartolomeo Campi, Pesaro 1546.

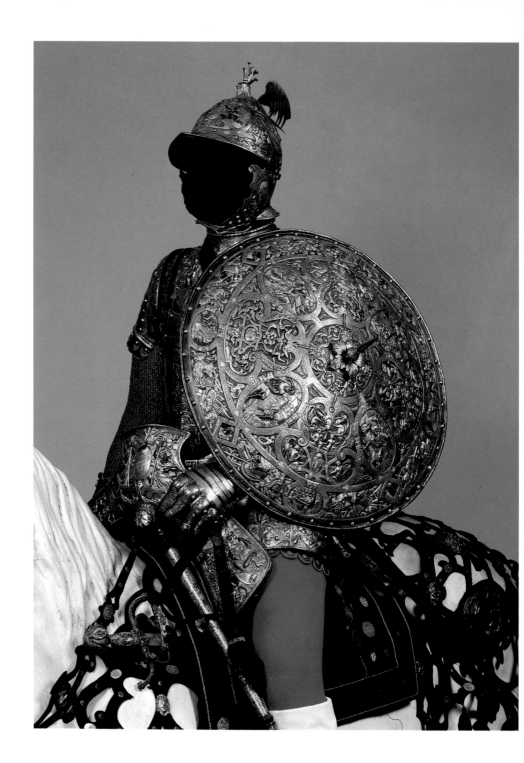

46 The 'Milanese armour' of the
Archduke Ferdinand II of Tyrol, by
Giovanni Battista Serabaglio and
Marc Antonio Fava.

He signed the parade armour for Charles v with the inscription BARTHOLOMEUS CAMPI AURIFEX . . . PERFECIT . . . PISAURI ANNO 1545, which shows clearly that he considered himself a goldsmith and not an armourer. Another highly decorated cuirass has survived in the Bargello at Florence and was probably made for Guidobaldo II of Urbino.

Another of the goldsmith-armourers was Giorgio Ghisi (1520–82) who also worked as an engraver. He was born in Mantua, but in 1540 he settled in Rome where he made a highly decorated shield which is now in the British Museum. The shield is signed GEORGIVS DE GHYSIS MANTVANVS 1554.

An armourer working in a very similar style to Bartolomeo Campi and Giorgio Ghisi was Filippo Negroli, who was active 1531–61. His real surname was Barini and he was highly praised by the two great Italian art historians Giorgio Vasari and Giovanni Paolo Lomazzo. Negroli always collaborated with his brother Francesco, a goldsmith and damascening artist, who is mentioned as Charles v's *dorador* and *deaurator* (gilder and goldsmith) in Milan. So the similarity of styles between Campi and Negroli is not surprising. On a shield which Filippo and Francesco Negroli made for Charles v at Madrid (Madrid D64) they signed PHILIPP. IACOBI. ET. F. NEGROLI FACIEBANT. MDXXXXI.

Very close in quality to the Negroli pieces is the armour made by Giovanni Battista Serabaglio (active 1560/70), an outstanding master of iron embossing, and Marc Antonio Fava (active 1560), the damascening artist. These two artists made an embossed, blued and gold- and silver-damascened garniture for Archduke Ferdinand II of Tyrol. Unfortunately, very little is known about the life of the embossing armourer Serabaglio, except that he signed himself *mercante*, so he must have been one of the merchant armourers who were so important for the armourers' trade in Milan. Equally fantastic are the works of another member of the Negroli family. Giovanni Paolo Negroli (active 1530–61) embossed elaborately decorated pieces of armour for the Habsburg family as well as for the Kings of France. Like Serabaglio, he forged an armour for Archduke Ferdinand II of Tyrol.

47 The Medusa shield of the Emperor Charles v by Filippo and Francesco Negroli, Milan 1541.

This armour *alla romana* consists primarily of mail but the helmet and the shoulder pieces are decorated with monsters beaten out of a single piece of metal. Lucio Piccinino (active 1570–89), who was one of the leading artists who worked embossed armour in Milan, is known from the book by Paolo Morigia *La nobilitá de Milano* (1595). In this book in praise of Milan, Paolo Morigia says that Lucio Piccinino was not only an armourer who embossed in iron, but that he acted also as a goldsmith. The one piece which we can certainly attribute to Lucio Piccinino is the parade armour of Duke Alexander Farnese. The surfaces of all these goldsmiths' armours are enriched by silver and gold damascening. A whole group of Italian embossed armours is attributed to Lucio Piccinino, but it is much more likely that they are the product of several Milanese goldsmith-armourers, of whom Lucio Piccinino was the most famous.

We know more about Gasparo Mola (*c*. 1590–1640). Like Leone Leoni, he was a highly versatile artist. He was primarily a goldsmith, but he also worked as a sculptor, a medallist and an armourer. In 1607 Gasparo Mola worked as goldsmith and medallist at the court of Charles Emmanuel I of Savoy in Turin. After 1609 he worked in Florence first as a goldsmith for Grand Duke Ferdinand I de Medici and then as an armourer for his successor Cosimo II. He made a helmet and a shield for Cosimo II which are now in the Bargello Museum (M760/761).

Less versatile than the Italian goldsmith armourers was the Augsburg goldsmith Jörg Sigman (1527–1601). About 1548 the armourer Desiderius Helmschmid employed Sigman to help him to decorate an armour for Prince Philip, later King Philip II of Spain. Most probably Sigman also cooperated with Anton Peffenhauser, the successful merchant armourer of Augsburg, who also produced an embossed armour for the King of Portugal. Sigman's excursions into the trade of the armourer brought him into trouble with the armourers' guild, which had to be solved by the intervention of Philip II of Spain. In 1552 he made an extremely fine round shield which is now in the Victoria and Albert Museum in London. It is

The left shoulder of the parade armour of the Duke Alexander Farnese, showing its embossed decoration. Large, grotesque masks are surrounded by *putti*, festoons of fruit, nude female figures and sphinxes interlaced with scrollwork.

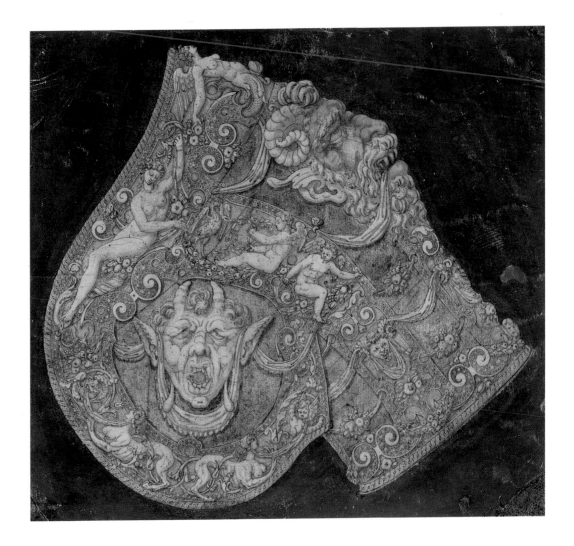

48 *Left* Parade armour of the Duke Alexander Farnese of Parma and Piacenza (1545–92) by Lucio Piccinino, Milan 1578.

43

50 The 'Roman armour' of the Archduke Ferdinand II of Tyrol by Giovanni Paolo Negroli (1530–61). Such armour was strictly for parade use and would never have been worn in combat.

signed GEORGIVS SIGMAN AVRIFEX AVGVSTE HOC
OPVS PERFECIT ANNO DOMINI MDLII. MENE AVGVST.
DIE XXVII.

Like Jörg Sigman, an Antwerp goldsmith
called Eliseus Libaerts (known to be active
1557–69) specialised in richly embossed armour. When Eric XIV came to the throne of
Sweden he ordered a series of highly decorated
armours from Libaerts. Documents show that
Libaerts was in Antwerp 1557–64. In 1564,
when Libaerts was on his way to visit the
Swedish King in Stockholm, his ship was
captured by order of the Danish King Frederick I
and Libaerts was taken prisoner. The two
garnitures for Eric XIV were captured with him,
and were later sold to Dresden. Eliseus Libaerts
entered the service of his captor and worked for
him until 1569 as a medallist. He most probably
also decorated the so-called 'Hercules armour'
for the Emperor Maximilian II, now in Vienna. In
all his works Eliseus Libaerts used the designs of
the French draughtsman and famous engraver
Etienne Delaune (1518/19–82); so did the
Parisian goldsmith Pierre Redon. In 1572 Redon
made a morion and a shield for the short-lived
French King Charles IX (1550–74). The embossed and chased gold is enriched by vitreous
enamels and semi-precious stones.

51 Embossed armour of Philip II of Spain made by
Desiderius Helmschmid and decorated by Jörg Sigman
in Augsburg in 1548.

52 *Left* Anton Peffenhauser made this embossed armour for a king of Portugal. It was probably decorated by Jörg Sigman.

53 *Below* Jörg Sigman made this round shield in Augsburg in 1552.

54 *Opposite* Parade armour of Erik XIV of Sweden (1533–77). The decoration was done by Eliseus Libaerts in Antwerp in 1560–3.

4 THE WEALTH OF THE ARMOURERS

It is not easy to evaluate the income of a 'normal' armourer, that is an independent craftsman who was unsalaried. Clearly, the price which he could charge for his work was a most important factor in his income, and we do know quite a lot about the price of armour.

Prices differed greatly depending upon the quality of the armour. They also changed considerably between the fifteenth century and the early seventeenth century. In 1441 Sir John Cressy bought a ready-made Milanese armour for £8.6s.8d, but in 1614 the armour of Prince Henry cost the astronomical sum of £340. This is a huge price rise, even when we consider the increase in labour costs (perhaps a doubling of wages over that period). The explanation pro-

bably lies in the fact that the 1441 armour was ready-made, whereas Prince Henry's was a fine, high-quality, made-to-measure suit. A tremendous amount of labour must have gone into the forging and decoration of such armour.

Great differences in price also occurred within the same decade. In August 1469 Lord John Howard paid Thomas Armourer of London 20 marks for two harnesses. (One mark = about 13s.4d.) In July 1463, however, he had paid only 5 marks for an armour which was complete except for sallet (helmet) and greaves; and in 1468 Lord Howard paid £6.16s.8d. for armour decorated with an ostrich feather.

In 1458, in Milan, Pier Innocenzo and his father promised to make Pietro Beaqua twelve

55 Vulcan forging a helmet. From the *Aeneid* of Heinrich von Waldec (now in Berlin).

harnesses for 32 lire each. In the same city eight years later Antonio Missaglia received a commission for a hundred harnesses for the ducal mercenaries at a price of 20,000 lire (ie 200 lire each). Missaglia was paid about seven times more per armour than Pier Innocenzo. Another Milanese armourer, Giacomo da Cantono, seems to have charged more for his products than Pier Innocenzo, but not as much as Missaglia. In 1483 he was owed 50 lire for a complete armour by Giovanni Antonio Forti. A year earlier another customer had owed him 700 lire for one hundred *corazzine* (literally 'little cuirasses', probably meaning brigandines) and one hundred *celatine* (helmets). This seems to be a ridiculously low price. In Germany in 1496 Jörg Helmschmid, one of Maximilian I's favourite armourers, received 100 florins for a helmet and a shaffron.

Munition armour seems to have been rather cheap in the early sixteenth century. Henry VIII, attempting to reorganise the English arsenal in the Tower of London, bought great quantities of munition armour. In 1512 he purchased two thousand light armours from Florence at 16 shillings each, and in 1513 a further five thousand from Milan. Under the threat of a French invasion in 1539 he purchased twelve hundred complete harnesses for £451 in Cologne, and another two thousand seven hundred for £630 in Antwerp. So in Cologne he paid a little over 7 shillings per harness and even less in Antwerp.

High-quality armour was, of course, far more expensive than munition armour, but again prices varied according to the type of armour and the reputation of the maker. In 1527 Hans Seusenhofer demanded 70 florins for an etched armour for field and tilt, 50 florins for a field armour and 25 florins for an etched half-armour. However, prices could be much higher than this. The Adler (Eagle) Garniture, one of the largest on record, was ordered by the later Emperor Ferdinand I for his younger son Archduke Ferdinand II of Tyrol from Jörg Seusenhofer of Innsbruck. It cost the enormous price of 1,258 florins. Even when we take into account the cost of the etched decoration, and the fact that the garniture consisted of eighty-seven different

56 The embossed 'Hercules armour' of Emperor Maximilian II by Eliseus Libaerts.

57 Splendid gold and enamel morion (open helmet) of Charles IX of France, made by Pierre Redon, the Paris goldsmith.

parts which could be assembled into twelve different armours for use in light horse combat, in the field, for tournaments and for foot combat, the price is still extraordinarily high. The sum of 1,258 florins was about twelve times the annual income of a high-ranking civil servant of that time. This amount does not even include the gilding, for which another 463 florins were charged. Ferdinand of Tyrol also commissioned the so-called *Mailander Rustung* (Milanese Armour) in 1559, an armour for light horse combat, which cost 2,400 *welsche* [Italian] *crouns*. This sum is far more than a simple artisan would have earned in a lifetime.

As we have seen, gilding formed a major component of the price of high-quality armour. In a letter of 1557 Andreas Brenker informed the Archduke Ferdinand of Tyrol that he would have to pay at least 400 florins for an armour, because the gilding (done by another craftsman) would cost him 100 ducats and the etcher would demand another 100 florins for his work. From this example, and that of the Eagle Garniture, we can see that payments to craftsmen other than the armourer himself accounted for a third to a half of the cost of high-quality armour. Armour was not always so fabulously expensive, however. In 1627 Emperor Ferdinand II paid 150 florins for a suit made by Hans Prenner.

Munition armour remained cheap in the first third of the seventeenth century. We are quite well informed about the prices of munition armour in Brunswick and Graz in the seventeenth century. In Brunswick armour cost between $2\frac{1}{4}$ and 4 taler depending on its type. In Graz (in Austria) a light armour for an infantryman might cost 7 florins but a full horseman's armour or field armour could cost between 35 and 150 florins.

Besides the price he could charge, the other important factors in an armourer's income were his costs. The bills of the court workshop in Innsbruck provide some indication of the cost structure of an armourer's workshop. Konrad Seusenhofer was allowed 1,000 florins to pay for the running of the royal workshop, including all the wages but excluding the costs of the raw materials, iron and steel. With this sum he had to pay six journeymen (who received one florin a

week) and four polishers (who were paid the same wage). There were also two apprentices who were paid half a florin a week each. We also know what Henry VIII paid his Almain armourers in the Royal Workshop in Greenwich. Erasmus, the chief armourer, got £17 per year; more junior armourers and the millmen got £15; locksmiths were paid £12; and the apprentices received £9. Altogether the royal workshop employed twelve armourers, two locksmiths, two millmen and four apprentices. Over and above their wages the armourers were given four yards of broadcloth and three yards of carsey for their clothing.

A freelance armourer would not necessarily have paid such high wages; the craftsmen at Innsbruck and Greenwich were highly qualified specialists in quality armour. Armourers employed at the arsenal in Graz, who did repair work most of the time, were paid 15 florins a year, whereas the armourer at the Brunswick arsenal got 30 florins a year plus one bushel of wheat. The system of paying wages partly 'in kind' was also used in Italy. A contract concluded on 6 October 1406 between the *magister ab armis* (armourer) Donato D'Arconate and the journeyman Giovanni da Celario states that the journeyman would get lodging and board free and receive a monthly wage of 2 soldi 16 imperiali.

Labour was one important cost factor in an armourer's workshop; another was the cost of his raw materials. We can find out something of the cost structure from the expenses of the Royal Armoury in Greenwich in 1544. The court workshop needed eight bundles of steel (see below) per year at a price of 38 shillings per bundle or £15 a year. It also needed forty-eight loads of charcoal at 9 shillings a load (more than £21 a year). It is very interesting that the cost of fuel should exceed the costs of iron and steel. We have to add to this the cost of buff leather, which could be up to £5 depending on its type.

The cost of iron seems to have fallen in 1544, because in 1516 four bundles of steel cost £8.6s.8d. However, this may be a false impression, because we know little about the origin of the two deliveries. In 1517, 2,541 lbs (1155 kg) of Innsbruck steel cost £26.12s. We don't know

58 Gold and enamel shield made by Pierre Redon for Charles IX, along with the morion illustrated on page 50.

exactly how much a 'bundle' weighed, but we can try to work it out using the two prices of 1516 and 1517. In 1516 a bundle cost about £2.10s. If we assume that the price of steel in 1517 was approximately the same, we can gather that a bundle of steel was about 264 lbs (120 kg).

The price of steel varied according to its origin. In 1562 a ton (2,240 lbs or 1,018 kg) of Spanish iron cost about £12; but in the same year an identical quantity of raw English iron cost £12.10s.

In Germany in the sixteenth and seventeenth centuries, steel and iron were usually delivered in so-called *säm*. One *säm* was the amount of steel which could be transported by one mule, ie about 140 kg or twenty steel plates. At that time a *säm* of steel cost between 10 and 12 florins.

From the expenses of the Royal Armoury in Greenwich we know that the workshop ordered 1,300 lbs (590 kg) of iron and 195 lbs (89 kg) of steel to forge thirty-two suits of armour. Therefore, each suit required nearly 41 lbs (18.5 kg) of iron and 6 lbs (about 3 kg) of steel. A little less steel was used to forge armour in Germany. As a suit weighed between 20 and 25 kg, an armourer could make between six and seven suits of armour out of one *säm* of steel. So the raw material costs for one suit of armour seem to have been between $1\frac{1}{2}$ and 2 florins.

In order to estimate the possible income of an armourer, we must take into account one final factor in addition to the selling prices and the workshop costs. That is the length of time it took to forge armour. This is rather difficult to assess, but it was obviously a lengthy period. The documents often speak of delays in the delivery of ordered armour. Obviously, the time it took to produce armour depended upon its quality. Munition armour was relatively quick to make. Production times were also affected by the manpower restrictions which the guilds imposed on armourers. Valentin Siebenbürger of Nüremberg made several demands for more journeymen in order to deliver on time. In 1468 or 1469 Louis XI, King of France, demanded that Gian Galeazzo Sforza, Duke of Milan, send him the master armourer Jacobino Ayroldo and twelve journeymen with their tools to make suits of armour for him. We know that in 1425 the Parisian armourer Thomassin de Froimont, who worked for Philip the Good, needed three and a half months to make two jousting armours for his master. In order to achieve this he was most certainly assisted by three or four journeymen. At the same time master Nicolas, court armourer of the Duke of Lorraine, forged two armours in three months.

The production time increased considerably when the armour was gilded and etched; Andreas Brenker's letter to Archduke Ferdinand II of Tyrol in 1557 states that the armourer needs six to seven months to forge an etched and gilded armour. To make a breastplate, a back, one helmet, a gorget and one shoulder he only demanded two months. Since the armourer thought he would need only one-third as much time to make half as much armour, it seems that about two months were needed by the etcher and gilder.

We know what the court armourers earned, since they were on fixed wages. They were certainly not the worst-paid armourers, but their income was far surpassed by the great master armourers. Konrad Seusenhofer, the court armourer of Maximilian I in Innsbruck, earned a yearly wage of 200 florins, which is about four times as much as his journeymen. Not all court armourers were so highly valued. A court armourer employed in Graz was paid roughly half as much as Seusenhofer. Even taking into account the costs of raw material and labour, the prices paid for high-quality armour were enormous, and the profits of the master armourers of Milan and Augsburg and Landshut must have been huge. They evidently became persons of wealth and importance. The enormous wealth of some of them is clear when we look at the huge debts which were owed to them by the European courts. All the courts liked to order expensive armour, but payment for these luxury items was often slow in coming, and the master armourers could exploit this to gain privileges from the ruling families. In 1450 Francesco Sforza, Duke of Milan, exempted Tommaso Missaglia from certain taxes. In 1451 Francesco Sforza owed Antonio Missaglia (son of Tom-

59 *Rennhut* helmet of Maximilian I made by Jörg Helmschmid, brother of the famous Lorenz Helmschmid.

60 *Below* Engraved shield made by H. Laubermann, Innsbruck, 1515. The design of the etching is attributed to Albrecht Dürer.

61 Part of the garniture 'de los mascarones' (decorated with grotesque masks) of Emperor Charles v by Filippo and Francesco Negroli, Milan 1539. Now in Madrid.

62 *Right* Kunz Lochner made this armour in Nuremberg, 1549. Its size, and the unusually long arms, indicate that it may have belonged to Archduke Ferdinand, later Emperor Ferdinand i (1503–64).

maso) 3,757 ducats; in 1452 the debt grew to 4,000 ducats and in 1453 to 25,000 lire (one *lira imperiale* was worth slightly more than one ducat). To judge just how big this debt was, we have to remember that in 1458 Pier Innocenzo got only 32 lire for one harness. In 1454 the duke repaid 13,659 lire, but in 1455 his debt to Antonio Missaglia mounted to 18,000 lire. Missaglia was recompensed with part of the taxes of Pavia. Duke Francesco Sforza's son Galeazzo Maria Sforza became even more heavily indebted than his father. At one time he owed the armourer as much as 100,000 lire! The fact that the company owned by Antonio Missaglia could survive and prosper with such vast debts unpaid is a testament to its financial strength.

The constant indebtedness of the dukes allowed the Missaglias to win great economic concessions. In 1467 Antonio was allowed to erect a polishing mill next to San Marco. In 1469 the Duke of Milan gave Antonio a mill near the S. Angelo Canal on the Naviglio dell Martesana, and in 1473 a mill near the Ponte Beatrice. In 1470 Antonio leased a rich iron mine near the forest of Canzo from the Ducal Chamber, and in 1472, in recognition of his services to the state and the chronic indebtedness of the duke, he was allowed to purchase the iron mine together with the furnace. In 1471/72 Missaglia exchanged a house on the Piazza Castello for a fief which was worth 15,200 lire. He thus rose into the class of the landed gentry. The vast wealth of the Missaglias had already opened the way into the aristocracy; in 1435 Tommaso Missaglia was knighted by Duke Filippo Maria Visconti.

The Missaglias were not the only wealthy master armourers. Franz Grosschedel of Landshut also received princely sums for his armour. In 1555 Prince Philip (later King of Spain) paid him an advance of 1,000 escudos plus a further 1,350 escudos on delivery of an armour. Philip's cousin, the Emperor Maximilian II, at one time owed Franz Grosschedel 2,250 florins. Another example was Anton Peffenhauser, one of the richest armourers of his time. Many of the nobles of Spain, Bavaria, Saxony and Austria ordered their splendid suits of armour from the Augsburg master. Great wealth led, as usual, to social advancement. In 1556 Anton Peffenhauser became a member of the great council of Augsburg.

Relations between a patron and his favourite armourer were close, and not only at the financial level. The great master armourers got fantastic prices for their work, but they were also rewarded by their princely customers with presents. Patrons also often ennobled their favourite armourers, and intervened on their behalf if they got into conflict with the city authorities. In 1526 Emperor Charles V gave Colman Helmschmid a present of 500 ducats to reward him for his toil and hardship while travelling to fit and alter armour for the Emperor. Desiderius Colman Helmschmid, who took over the workshop from his father in 1532, also rose in the social hierarchy of the city of Augsburg. In 1550 he became a member of the city council and in 1556 he was made Court Armourer by Charles V. The title was later confirmed by Maximilian II.

63 The armourer. This woodcut comes from Jost Amman's *Stände und Handwerker, c.*1590.

5
THE PROCESS OF
MAKING ARMOUR

As mentioned in the Introduction, no medieval treatise on the making of armour has survived. However, something can be discovered from the few surviving documents, even when the sources are patchy and indirect. Correspondence between armourers and their customers provides some clues. Better sources of information on the art of armour-making are the contemporary illustrations of armourers at work. These can be found throughout the period covered by this book, beginning with the illustration of Vulcan forging a helmet in the Berlin *Aeneid* of Heinrich von Waldec (Codex MS Germ. fol. 282 p. 79) from the thirteenth century, and ending with the etchings of Jost Amman in his book on craftsmen *Stände und Handwerker* (1590).

MAIL

As we saw in the Introduction, mail was the earliest kind of metal armour to be developed, and it remained in widespread use for centuries. In Europe mail was made until the end of the seventeenth century, as we know from an engraving by Christoph Weigel (1698). The craft survived as late as the twentieth century in the Sudan, where it was recorded by the historian Arkell. It may seem surprising that mail should dominate the history of armour manufacture for such a long time, almost outliving plate armour. The reason probably lies in its special advantages: it was easy to produce, flexible to wear, and provided good protection against cutting blows. Its fatal disadvantage was the limited protection it offered against missile weapons such as the crossbow.

The craft of making mail is quite separate and distinct from that of manufacturing plate armour. Because so much mail was produced, the method of manufacture must have been fast, allowing for division of labour within the workshop. The most skilled task, the final

64 A mail-maker, drawn in the late seventeenth century by Christopher Weigel (in the *Ständebuch*).

56

linking, must have been done by the master craftsman, who would have been kept supplied with the necessary rings and rivets. The early stages in the production of mail – the simple, laborious tasks – were left to apprentices and assistants. Such a system was often found in small workshops.

There were two possible methods of producing the rings of mail. Closed rings were probably made by punching them from a plate of metal with a double punch or by punching a single hole and trimming the outside. Open rings were usually made from iron wire. There has been much controversy as to whether or not the ancient mail-maker knew the art of wire-drawing. In this process a forged rod is drawn through successively smaller and smaller swages (holes). Another method is to cut the wires from a thin sheet of iron and then file, scrape and hammer them into the appropriate shape. A combination of both methods was to cut a strip from a larger sheet (about 3 to 5 mm thick) and then draw the strip down to the required diameter through a lesser number of successively smaller holes. It is likely that this is how small-diameter iron and steel wire was produced in the days when it was difficult to produce a hot rod in sections small enough for wire-drawing. The length of wire would be wound round a rod of the diameter of the required ring, producing a long coil. The coil was then cut up one side from end to end, producing a number of rings.

In all the processes so far described the rings could be worked cold, but as soon as the metal became hard through working it had to be annealed (heated until it was softened). To accomplish this it was brought to red heat and left to cool. This heating would be necessary every now and then while drawing the wire and before the open rings were overlapped. A mail-maker would thread the rings on a length of wire and heat them in the forge. For overlapping, the rings were driven through a tapering hole in a steel block with a punch. Ideally the rings would be annealed again after the overlapping so that they were quite soft before the next stage. This was the flattening of the ends of the rings. The flattened, overlapped ends were punched or

65 A German mail shirt from the mid-fifteenth century.

66 The wire drawer. From the *Hausbuch der Mendelschen Zwolfbrüderstiftung*, 1435–6 (see caption to figure 7).

67 *Above* A mail-maker. From Jost Amman's *Stände und Handwerker*, c.1590.

68 *Right* Armourers at work (though hardly in a realistic setting!). A manuscript illumination from Boccaccio's *Les clercs et nobles femmes*, early 15th century.

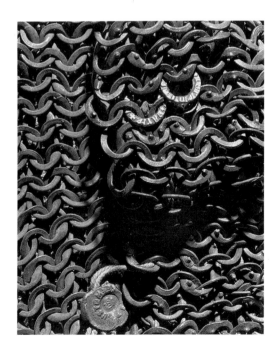

bored with holes for rivets. The rivets were always of iron even if the rings were brass, and they were usually wedge-shaped. The rivet backs were rectangular, while the fronts must have come to a point originally (before the rivet was closed). The rivets were made out of wire. The wire was hammered out at one end into a fan shape and then cut to a point with wire-cutters. This produced a four-sided end, tapering on all sides. This tapering end was now cut from the rest of the wire to form a rivet.

The mail-maker would assemble the rings so that they were interlinked, each ring passing through four others. When the mail-maker used closed rings he arranged them in alternate rows with open rings. The pierced ends of the open rings were overlapped and a small rivet inserted. This was burred over with a hammer or with punches as is shown in the illustration 'The Mail-maker' from Jost Amman's *Stände und Handwerker*. There is also an interesting miniature in the manuscript of Boccaccio's *Des clercs et nobles femmes* (Bib. Reg. 16. G fol. 11) in the British Library which shows a seated man closing up the mail rings with a pair of pincers. The same kind of riveting pincers can also be observed in the illustrations from the *Hausbuch der Mendelschen Zwölfbrüderstiftung*. An engraving in Weigel's *Ständebuch* shows these riveting pincers still in use as late as 1689. The closing of the rings could also be achieved by hammer welding.

When assembling the rings the mail-maker used a pattern which must have resembled a modern knitting pattern. Sadly none of these patterns have survived, but we know that garments of mail were shaped by adding or leaving out extra rings in each row. Occasionally, to create a stronger mail shirt, two rings were used for every one of the ordinary mail; or sometimes the garment was rolled up in charcoal and case-hardened.

Some mail rings bear armourer's marks. For example, there is a German mail shirt in the Tower of London, into which are woven three brass rings. The first is marked with the maker's name *bertolt parte* (Bertolt Parte) and the second with the name of his town *to isrenloen* (Iserlohn in Westphalia). Bertholt came from a family of

wire-drawers and is known to have worked between 1390 and 1450. In the Metropolitan Museum of Art in New York there is a mail shirt with a small label riveted to it. This label bears the stamp of Nüremberg.

PLATE ARMOUR

The manufacture of plate armour was a complicated business which demanded the cooperation of a number of specialised craftsmen: the armourer who forged the plates (in the Royal Armouries at Greenwich they were called 'hammermen'); the polisher (or 'millman') who polished the shaped plates; and the finisher who was responsible for assembling the whole armour properly and fitting its strappings and linings, padding and leather gloves. In larger workshops, like the Greenwich armouries, locksmiths were employed to make the hinges and fastenings of the armour. Most armourers could not afford to employ a locksmith, however, so they bought their hinges and fastenings from large specialist merchants. After all this work, fine armour was still not finished; the decorative artists, the etchers, gilders and painters, would complete it.

Plate armour was made from billets of steel or wrought iron. These billets had to be hammered into flat plates. Although at first all the hammerwork was done by hand, later the preliminary work was probably carried out by a water-driven tilthammer, like the one shown in *Venus at the Forge of Vulcan*, a Flemish painting by Jan Breughel and H. van Balen. Perhaps the water-powered rolling mills which were being used in the Liege district and in Germany to make iron bars as early as 1500 were also used to produce plates of iron. There seems little doubt that this method was being used to produce metal sheets at least by the middle of the sixteenth century. The process is first described in 1615, but rolled plates do not seem to have been produced in any significant quantity until the second quarter of the seventeenth century, when they were employed for the manufacture of munition armour.

The hammering of billets into plates could be done by the armourer himself, but in most cases it was done at the iron-producing centre and the iron or steel arrived at the workshop in the form of plates. Although most of the great centres of armour manufacture were situated in iron-bearing districts, a brisk export trade existed from Germany, Lombardy and Spain to less fortunate areas.

The plates were then cut into shapes suitable for the various pieces of armour, which were made by hammering the shaped plates over the appropriate metal formers or stakes (like those used by modern silversmiths). These were small anvils of various shapes, each mounted on a vertical bar that could be fitted into a hole in the armourer's workbench or into a large wooden block kept for this purpose. A woodcut in the *Weisskunig* of Hans Burgkmaier shows Konrad Seusenhofer's bench littered with these little anvils or stakes. The 1514 inventory of the Greenwich court workshop listed all the different stakes. There was a *pype stake* (a round-horned anvil for making tubes), a *creste stake* (for beating up a helmet crest), a *vysure stake* (for visors), a *curace stake* (for the cuirass) and a *stake for the hedde pecys* (for forging helmets). Together with the various stakes there were special hammers. A *platynge hamer* was a heavy hammer, maybe a sledge hammer. There were numerous smaller hammers: a *hamer for the hedde pecys*, a *creste hamer*, a *greve hamer*, a *reweting hamer* (for rivets) and a *boos hamer* (for the embossing of steel or iron).

The metal seems to have been worked cold for the basic shaping of the plate, as is shown in illustrations such as Burgkmaier's *Weisskunig* or the *Hausbuch der Mendelschen Zwölfbrüderstiftung*. In both of these the armourers are shown working the metal held in their bare hands, and therefore it must be cold. But there is no doubt that it was annealed frequently during the process. The forge in the background of the *Weisskunig* illustration stands ready for this purpose. To anneal a steel of normal quality the metal was heated to a fairly high temperature, perhaps as high as a red heat, and then allowed to cool slowly.

Heat was also required for some details like turned-over edges. The edges of parts which were going to form the outer edge of a defence were stiffened by bending the plate round a

71 *Previous pages: Venus at the Forge of Vulcan* by Jan Brueghel and H. Van Balen, Flemish school, *c*.1620. I.38.

62

wire. The raised metal plate formed a stop rib to prevent a weapon glancing off the edge into a vital part, and also made the edge less liable to damage. Prior to the forming of the edges the borders of the finished plate were trimmed by means of a huge pair of shears, fixed in a heavy block of wood to keep them steady. Such a pair of shears can be seen in the *Weisskunig* woodcut of the court armoury.

In fine armour great care was taken to see that the metal was thickest over the most vulnerable spots. The thickness of the pieces varied, not only between different plates but in different parts of the same plate. A breastplate was thicker than a backplate, but the breastplate itself was also thicker in the centre than round the sides. The front part of a helmet was generally thicker than the back. Also, the left side of good-quality armour was often made heavier than the right, because the left was the side turned towards an enemy.

The hardness of the surface of armour also varied. Much plate armour was case-hardened, leaving the outside diamond-hard while the inside remained as soft as the original iron. The process of case-hardening was described by Theophilus the Monk in the twelfth century. In his compilation *De Diversis Artibus* (On Diverse Arts) he described how iron files were hardened. To harden iron it must at least in part be converted to steel. For this Theophilus suggested smearing the iron with old hog's lard. The iron was then wrapped in strips of goatskin covered in clay and heated for a considerable time. Carbon would very slowly diffuse into the iron, increasing the carbon content of the piece. The amount and depth of penetration naturally depended upon the length of time that the hot iron and carbon (or organic material) remained in contact. The absorption of carbon would be greatest at the surface but gradually this layer of steel would deepen as the process continued, until eventually the iron became steel right through. A more efficient form of case-hardening involved surrounding the piece of iron with crushed charcoal and packing it tightly in an iron box. The box was placed in the forge and kept at red heat for some time.

Steel may also have been made by a more

72 *Right* An armourer hammering out a breastplate from the *Hausbuch der Mendelschen Zwölfbrüderstiftung*, 1533.

73 Minerva visits an armourer's workshop, c.1460, grisaille by Guillaume Vreland. One armourer works on a plate with a hammer; he is using his bare hand, so the plate must be cold. The second armourer is polishing. A forge stands ready to anneal the metal.

direct method, which was in use for a long time in certain areas of Europe. Styria was an ancient centre of iron-making and the furnace there may have been operated to make steel in this way. In this method the bloom (piece of newly made iron) was not permitted to cool but left in the furnace longer, exposed to hot carbon monoxide gas from the burning charcoal. The result was iron of greater carbon content (ie steel). However, the resulting steel bloom did not have a consistent carbon content and therefore lacked consistent strength and hardness. A long process of folding and reforging was necessary to distribute the carbon content more evenly throughout the plate. This process was developed by the swordsmiths of medieval Japan, but it is probable that it was also used in Europe.

Steel is harder and stronger than iron; it also has the advantage that its hardness can be increased even further by *quenching*. This means plunging red-hot steel into a colder medium. The more rapidly the steel is cooled, the harder it becomes. High-carbon steel can be made practically glass-hard, but it also becomes exceedingly brittle. Water provides the most rapid cooling; if hot steel is quenched in oil, molten lead or air it will be less hard but also less brittle. The earliest mention of an oil quenching is in the works of the Byzantine lexicographer Suidas (976 AD). A better way to make hard, but not brittle, steel is to quench it in water and then reheat it very carefully to *temper* it. Tempering reduces most of the internal stress and therefore the brittleness. This modern two-stage method of hardening and tempering steel is described for the first time in the sixteenth century. In 1532 a German recipe book includes such a procedure, and a fuller description of tempering a coat of mail is to be found in the slightly later *Natural Magick* of Della Porter (1589).

The success of the tempering process depended upon the armourer's ability to control the temperature and to measure the time accurately. Because of the lack of clocks and thermometers, tempering demanded much experience; reheating the piece too much would reverse the hardening effect of the quenching, and reheating too little would leave it brittle. So the necessary techniques of hardening and then tempering steel correctly were closely guarded trade secrets.

In the tempering operation the degree of hardness which the steel retains is relative to the temperature at which the process is carried out. The lower the temperature, the less the hardness of the metal will be reduced. One method of controlling the temperature was to observe the colour of the metal during heat treatment. A portion of the surface of a piece of steel would be polished and the steel heated over a smokeless fire. During this heating process successive changes in the colour of the steel would occur. The bright steel would change to a straw colour, then brown, then blue, etc. Each of these tints represented a definite temperature and thus a state of hardness of the metal. So if the metal was quenched at a particular colour, it would retain a predictable degree of hardness.

However, this two-stage method of quenching and tempering was not generally employed in the Middle Ages. The one-stage process of *slack-quenching* was popular as a compromise solution to the problem of heat treatment. Slack-quenching might involve the use of a less drastic quenchant than water, or armourers might use delayed or interrupted quenching. The Milanese armourers used slack-quenching even though their pieces were thus of inferior quality to a fully quenched and tempered steel. The best of the Innsbruck and Augsburg masters seem to have known the two-stage process, which would explain the superior hardness of their products. Hardness was vital in plate armour. It prevented longbow arrows or crossbow bolts from penetrating, and even a shattering blow from axe or sword would glance off a sufficiently hard, smooth and rounded surface.

The various techniques for increasing the protective qualities of armour led to the development of *armour of proof*, which is known from the middle of the fourteenth century, and was very common in the fifteenth, sixteenth and especially the seventeenth centuries. Armour of proof was guaranteed to resist contemporary weapons. At first, it was tested by means of crossbow shots. In the sixteenth century, when firearms became a serious factor in warfare, the armour was submitted to pistol or musket shot.

74 A polisher finishing armour by hand, from the *Hausbuch der Mendelschen Zwölfbrüderstiftung*, 1483.

75 This later illustration shows a polisher using a water-driven polishing mill. From the *Hausbuch der Mendelschen Zwölfbrüderstiftung*, 1571.

The dents caused by the testing bullets are frequently to be seen on seventeenth-century breastplates. In the seventeenth century armour was mostly made out of wrought iron, so the required superior strength could not be achieved through hardening. The only way of making it 'proof' was to make it thicker. This had the disadvantage of making it so heavy that troops were increasingly unwilling to wear it.

After the pieces of a harness had been forged with the hammer they would be fitted together and assembled temporarily. This was the most difficult part of the whole process of armour manufacture. The exact fit of all the single pieces was of the greatest importance, for if the various parts did not fit snugly over or under each other, the armour would not work flexibly and dangerous gaps would appear as the wearer moved. If necessary the pieces were filed until they fitted properly. When this was done the parts would go to the polisher or millman. At this point the pieces would still be blackened from the fire, covered with dimple marks from the hammer blows, and rough at the edges. Polishers, who smoothed the outside and pol- 75 ished the surface mirror-bright on swiftly rotating, water-powered grindstones, were often employed by the bigger armourers' workshops. The Innsbruck court workshop employed two millmen as well as six journeymen; so did the Royal Armoury at Greenwich. As the pictures in the *Hausbuch der Mendelschen Zwölf-* 74 *brüderstiftung* illustrate, much of the early polishing was done by hand. Only the richer polishers or the great master armourers could afford the water- or horse-driven polishing wheels.

The pieces of armour then went back from the polisher to the master armourer who assembled them in the right order. The plates were attached to each other by means of rivets. Each one of the *lames* (the small joining plates) was riveted to a leather strap running along the edge of the main armour plate on the inside. Then hinges and buckles were applied. At first, brass hinges were riveted onto the outside of the plates, but later on internal steel hinges were used because they were less exposed to damage in action. Of course, armour had to open and close so that the owner could get it on and off.

Buckles were the earliest form of fastening, but in the sixteenth century it was more usual to have a staple on the inner plate which fitted a hole in the outer. The staple was pierced so that the point of a pin or a hook (fixed to the outer plate) could be hooked through the staple, preventing the plates from coming apart.

The completed armour was fitted with a padded lining inside the helmet, the breastplate, the tassets and the upper part of the leg. During the second half of the sixteenth century and the seventeenth century the lining usually extended beyond the edges of the plates as a series of tabs of coloured velvet, known as *pickadils*. These prevented the plates from scratching.

Although harnesses could be bought ready-made from merchants, the wealthy normally ordered them from an armourer specialising in fine quality work. Great care was taken to ensure that the armour fitted its owner. Producing a high-quality armour was a first-class tailoring job. Getting accurate measurements from their clients could be a problem for armourers. In some cases customers sent items of clothing as a pattern. In at least one case the garment was specially made for the purpose. In 1386 the Duke of Touraine bought three ells of fine linen of Reims to have a little doublet made to be sent to a German armourer. Just sending clothes had some disadvantages, as we learn from a letter from Andreas Brenker to Archduke Ferdinand II. Brenker quotes the master armourer Konrad Richter, who was most willing to make an armour for the Archduke, but insisted that although he could deduce the length and width of the customer from his garments, he could not see if his neck was long or short or if his feet were straight or curved. Therefore, he wanted to fit the pieces on the Archduke himself before he hardened them, because afterwards alterations would be difficult.

Clearly, the best method was to take the measurements from the body of the customer. In 1464 the great Milanese armourer Francesco Missaglia stayed at the court of Burgundy to take measurements *sur le corps de mondit seigner* (from the body of the customer) before the armour was forged in Italy. Because it was considered so important to ensure an accurate fit, the process of obtaining measurements could take extreme forms. In 1466 Missaglia visited the French King Louis XI. The king asked Missaglia several times to go into his room and study him by day and night, even when he was going to bed, so that he might construct an armour that would not hurt the delicate body of the monarch.

At least one source suggests that master armourers might have kept models of the limbs of their favourite clients, not unlike fashionable shoemakers today. An entry in the accounts of the royal house of Spain in the late sixteenth century records wax for making models of the Emperor's legs; the models were probably sent to Charles V's favourite armourer, Desiderius Colman Helmschmid of Augsburg.

THE DECORATION OF ARMOUR

Almost all fine-quality armour was decorated, as we have already noted. We shall now look at the different means of decoration and how they were applied.

Engraving is by far the most ancient type of metal decoration, practised from the Middle Ages to the end of the age of armour. It is a mechanical process, in which the artist incises the lines of the design with a sharply pointed tool. It is laborious and difficult, unlike the (technically more complicated) process of chemical etching with acid, so relatively little engraving appears on armour.

From the beginning of the thirteenth century (or earlier) until the early sixteenth century armourers decorated their work with gilding and painting. The gilding was either applied by firing or as painter's gilding. In the first process, an amalgam containing mercury was applied to the surface of the plate to make the gold adhere to the metal. Heat was then applied in order to evaporate or 'fume off' the mercury. This process is highly toxic, so most of the gilders must have been short-lived. The second process was gilding with leaf gold. The surface of the plate was painted with a varnish which was allowed to dry for twenty-four hours. Then very finely beaten gold leaf was applied with a paint brush. Finally the decorated plate was heated gently to dry the varnish completely and secure

76 This engraved and gilt armour belonged to Charles I (1600–49). Dutch, *c*.1612. London, Royal Armouries.

the adhesion of the gold. In 'painter's gilding', gold dust was dissolved in varnish and brushed over the surface. In the late Middle Ages the decorative artists sometimes painted the armour with patterns of bands or squares, and sometimes with heraldic devices. For this they used some kind of oil-based paint.

Another method of colouring armour was the 'tint' method. Particularly in the fifteenth century, many armourers heat-blued the surface of plate armour. This bluing gave the highly-polished surface a certain amount of protection from rust and also offered an opportunity for colourful decoration. As mentioned above, bright steel changes colour when heated. To obtain a deep blue the armourer had to heat the steel to 310 degrees Celsius and then quench it immediately. In 1477 Lorenz Helmschmid used the blued surface of a horse-barde made for the Emperor Frederick III as a background for his decoration. The decorative pattern was painted onto the blued metal with an acid-resistant varnish. Then the surface was etched with a mild acid (probably warm vinegar). The acid was sufficiently strong to remove the bluing but it did not eat into the metal. The method of heat-bluing was also used by the artist who decorated the (restored) blue and gold parade armour of Emperor Maximilian II (1527–76). It is one of the last armours to be decorated with applied gilded metal borders. The unknown Augsburg armourer who forged this garniture for Maximilian II in 1557 used a form of decoration which was especially popular in the fourteenth and fifteenth centuries. The applied strips were of gilt bronze with Renaissance ornament, in contrast to the gilded silver and brass borders of the late Middle Ages, but it was still essentially an old-fashioned form of decoration. The narrow borders of gilded metal were riveted to the surface of the armour; this was the main form of decoration for late Gothic armour, like the suit made for Archduke Siegmund of Tyrol by Lorenz Helmschmid.

A technique which was used to decorate a few German armours from the late fifteenth century until *c.* 1530 is the so-called *Goldschmelz*. This gives armour a look of great luxury. Very shallow patterns were etched on the blued and polished surface. Then the etched surface was covered with a thin coating of copper to facilitate the amalgamation of gold and iron. Then the gilder applied gold amalgam to the prepared surface. Under heat the mercury in the amalgam was fumed off to leave the gold adhering to the steel. The gilded ornament showed up particularly well against the deep blue colour of the steel.

The most popular form of decoration, without any doubt, was etching. Blackened etched patterns were certainly used by Italian craftsmen in the fifteenth century to decorate their armour. We know from Italian books that the method was known as early as the late fourteenth century, but the earliest surviving examples of etched armour are from the fifteenth. The plate was first completely covered with a protective coating of acid-resistant varnish, oil paint, wax or even tar. Then the design was scratched away with an etching needle. The etcher would dip the plate into acid, which ate into the uncovered areas, cutting the design into the metal. Then the coating of varnish was washed away with turpentine. The etched design was blackened with a mixture of lamp-black and oil and the plate heated until the oil evaporated. Although this method was already used by the Italian craftsmen of the late Middle Ages, it was brought to its utmost perfection by the German etchers of the sixteenth century. Frequently these etchers copied their decoration from 60 published designs. Artists like Dürer, Holbein and the elder and younger Burgkmaiers produced designs for etched decoration on armour.

Many of the artists were closely connected with the armourers. Their collaboration could even result in family ties: Hans Burgkmair the Elder of Augsburg (1472–1559), for instance, married a sister of the famous armourer Colman Helmschmid (1470–1532) (who also bought the house of Helmschmid's widow), and Jörg Sorg the Elder (1522–1603) married Helmschmid's daughter Katharina. The artist Daniel Hopfer (active 1470–1536) is probably better known for his prints than for his armour, but he signed and etched a number of armours. It even seems that he was among the first to use the technique of etching iron plates not just for the decoration

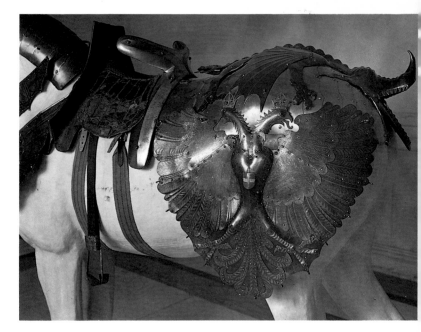

of armour but also for reproducing his designs in print.

In the second decade of the sixteenth century, the German etchers adopted a different technique. In their method the decoration was painted onto the metal with an acid-resistant varnish. Then the etcher would use a needle to scratch the fine details. The surface was etched with a strong acid which ate away the background area, leaving the design in slight relief on a deeply etched ground. The background was usually, but not always, decorated with small raised dots which might be gilded or blackened. For the Polish market the Nüremberg master armourer Kunz Lochner used an exquisite form of etched decoration. Today only two examples of this technique are known, the armour for horse and man of Sigismund II 25 August, King of Poland and the armour for his brother-in-law Nikolaus Radziwill. Unfortunately it has not been possible up to now to discover the name of the artist who worked for Lochner and etched the surfaces with an entwined ribbon pattern, which he then gilded and varnished in black, white and red. This 'cold enamel' replaced genuine enamel which, owing

77 *Above* Horse barde in the form of a double-headed eagle, made for the Emperor Frederick II by Lorenz Helmschmid.

78 *Right* Blued and gilded parade armour of Maximilian II (1527–96), Augsburg 1557 (restored).

79 *Far right* Late gothic armour of Archduke Siegmund of Tyrol (1427–96), by Lorenz Helmschmid, Augsburg c.1480.

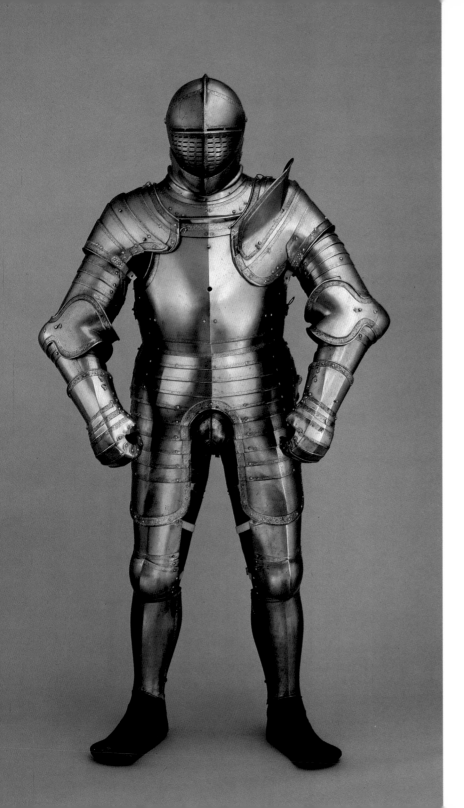

to its brittleness, was hardly suitable for armour. In spite of this disadvantage it was sometimes used; in 1572 the French goldsmith Pierre Redon used genuine enamel to decorate a parade shield and helmet for Charles IX.

Other, especially refined, techniques were employed by the goldsmith armourers for their fabulous works of art. One method was gold and silver damascening. In struck damascening, gold and silver foils were hammered into the roughened steel surface. In beaten damascening, patterns were cut into the steel with an engraving tool. Gold and silver wire was hammered into these grooves and the surface ground and polished.

The goldsmith armourers also specialised in the art of embossing. However, the oldest surviving armour with embossed decoration was the work of the Augsburg armourer Lorenz Helmschmid. In 1477 he made the horse barde for Emperor Frederick III in the Vienna Hofjagd- und Rüstkammer. The front plate on this is shaped and embossed to represent the demi-figure of an angel. The relief decoration was done with hammers and chisels in several stages.

The decoration of armour sometimes had to be approved by the customer; some small plates are preserved in the Real Armeria, Madrid, which show alternative designs to be used in the decoration of armour. They were sent from Germany to King Philip II of Spain so that he could make his final choice and decide which of the available techniques were to be used to decorate his armour. It was, in the end, the patron who was the most important person of all in the manufacture of medieval fine armour.

80 Part of Henry VIII's armour garniture, made in the royal workshop at Greenwich and dated 1540. London, Royal Armouries.

anneal To heat a metal hardened by cold working (eg hammering) until it is softened.

armour of proof An armour proven to be safe against contemporary weapons.

bacinet A form of head defence, generally egg-shaped with a pointed apex, which evolved in the fourteenth century when it was usually fitted with a pivoted visor either of rounded profile or pointed.

bloom or bloomery iron Iron that has been produced in a solid condition directly as a result of the reduction (eg melting) of iron ore. Pure iron melts at 1535°C, but bloomery iron usually has never been heated above about 1250°C.

case-hardening A method described in the twelfth century treatise *On Diverse Arts* by Theophilus the Monk) for hardening the surface of wrought iron by packing it in charcoal or other organic material and heating it for hours above 900°C.

cerveller A steel skull cap worn under the coif of mail or helmet.

cuirass The combined back- and breast-plates.

damascening A decorative technique in which gold or silver was used to enrich the surface of metalworking.

embossing The decoration of metal in relief by working it out of the plane with hammers and assorted chisels.

engraving The mechanical application of ornament to metal, using a steel burin or graver to cut the pattern in the surface.

etching A chemical method of applying ornament. The metal surface is covered with an acid-resistant varnish with the pattern being either left clear or scratched through to the metal

with a needle. Applied acid eats into the uncovered surface to leave a pattern that can be blackened, gilded or coloured.

garniture The armour garniture consists of an armour (or armours) and its 'double pieces', the reinforcing plates used to adapt the basic unit for various uses in the field and several forms of military sport.

gorget Defence for the neck, throat and upper thorax, generally formed of several lames each in two parts front and rear.

greave A plate defence for the lower leg, extending from below the knee to the ankle, or in some forms to the base of the heel.

harness A generic term for armour to protect the body and/or the limbs.

hauberk The long coat of mail that was the principal defence of the knights of the eleventh to thirteenth centuries.

horse barde Horse armour.

lames Metal plates that overlap to form a flexible defence.

mail The network of interlinked metal rings used to make extremely flexible defensive garments.

munition armour Mass-produced, cheaply made armour for the common soldier, produced in very large quantities.

price decree Edict which fixed maximum prices.

quench To cool a heated steel by plunging it into a colder medium. The more rapidly the steel is cooled, the harder it becomes.

sallet A form of helmet used in sport and war. In its classic German form of *c.* 1480 it is the most graceful of all head defences, extending backwards in a long tail.

shaffron The armour for a horse's head.

slack-quench To cool heated steel less rapidly than by plunging it into cold water.

tasset A metal plate or plates hung from the lowest skirt-plate to protect the thigh.

temper To soften the hard and brittle steel by heating it for a short time at temperatures between 100 and 650°C.

tint A slight colouring produced when polished steel is heated over a smokeless fire.

FURTHER READING

The literature on the medieval armourer is extensive, but patchy and scattered. Most recent research has focused on the armour and not on the armourers, but the non-specialist reader will find a number of valuable hints about the manufacture of armour in books such as:

C. BLAIR,
European Armour, London 1958.

HOWARD L. BLACKMORE,
Arms and Armour, New York 1965.

A. V. B. NORMAN,
Arms and Armour, London 1964.

A. V. B. NORMAN,
Warrior to Soldier, London 1964.

R. EWART OAKESHOTT,
A Knight and his Armour, London 1961.

DAVID EDGES & JOHN MILES PADDOCK,
Arms and Armour of the Medieval Knight, London 1988.

Besides these books there are a number of specialist articles dealing with certain groups of armourers or single craftsmen. A selection are listed below:

C. BLAIR,
'The Armourers' Bill of 1581: The Making of Arms and Armour in Sixteenth-Century London' in *The Journal of the Arms and Armour Society*, 1986.

'Greenwich Armour' in *Greenwich and Lewisham Antiquarian Society Transactions*, London 1985.

A. BRUHN DE HOFFMAIER,
'Arms and Armour in Spain, A Short Survey' Vol I In *Gladius* 1972, Vol II in *Gladius* 1982.

E. M. BURGESS,
'The Mail-Maker's Technique' in *The Antiquaries Journal*, 1953

F. H. CRIPPS-DAY,
Fragmenta Armentaria: An Introduction to the Study of Greenwich Armour, London 1934–45.

CHARLES FFOULKES,
The Armourer and his Craft, London 1912.

'The Armourers' Company of London and the Greenwich School of Armourers' in *Archaeologia*, London 1926.

'The Armourers of Italy' in *The Connoisseur*, London 1909.

'Some Aspects of the Craft of the Armourer' in *Archaeologia*, 1928.

O. GAMBER,
'Armour Made in the Royal Workshops at Greenwich: Style and Construction' in *Arms and Armours, Scottish Art Review*, 1969.

S. GRANCSAY,
'Lucio Piccinino: Master Armourer of the Renaissance' in *The Metropolitan Museum of Art Bulletin*, New York 1969.

J. F. HAYWARD,
'Filippo Orsoni, Designer and Caremolo Modrone, Armourer of Mantua' in *Zeitschrift der Gesellschaft für historische Waffen- und Kostümkunde*, 1982.

H. NICKEL,
'The Armourer's Shop' in *The Metropolitan Museum of Art Bulletin*, New York 1969.

A. V. REITZENSTEIN,
'Anton Peffenhauser: Last of the Great Armourers' in *Arms and Armour Annual* ed. Robert Held, 1973.

JEAN-PIERRE REVERSEAU,
'The classification of French Armour by Workshop Styles 1500–1600' in *Arms and Armour Annual* ed. Robert Held 1979.

C. S. SMITH,
'Methods of Making Chain Mail 14th–18th Centuries: A Metallographic Note' in *Technology and Culture*, 1959.

A. W. F. TAYLERSON,
'The London Armoury Company' in *The Journal of the Arms and Armour Society*, 1956.

A. R. WILLIAMS,
'The Knight and the Blast Furnace' in *Historical Metallurgy*, 1986.

'Medieval Metalworking – Armour Plate and the Advance of Metallurgy' in *Chartered Mechanical Engineer*, 1968.

PHOTOGRAPHIC CREDITS

INDEX